On Naming the Present

Concilium is an international theological journal begun in 1965. Inspired by the Second Vatican Council and the spirit of reform and dialogue which the Council inaugurated, *Concilium* has featured many of the world's foremost theologians. The *Concilium Series*, published by Orbis Books and SCM Press, highlights the contributions of these distinguished authors as well as selected themes that reflect the journal's concern for the mystical-political meaning of the Gospel for our age.

Already published

Edward Schillebeeckx, *The Language of Faith*

Johann-Baptist Metz and Jürgen Moltmann, *Faith and the Future*

CONCILIUM SERIES

DAVID TRACY

On Naming the Present

*Reflections on God,
Hermeneutics, and Church*

ORBIS BOOKS

Maryknoll, New York 10545

SCM PRESS

The Catholic Foreign Mission Society of America (Maryknoll) recruits and trains people for overseas missionary service. Through Orbis Books, Maryknoll aims to foster the international dialogue that is essential to mission. The books published, however, reflect the opinions of their authors and are not meant to represent the official position of the society.

Copyright © 1994 by the Concilium Foundation, Nijmegen, The Netherlands
Published by Orbis Books, Maryknoll, New York 10545, U.S.A., and SCM Press, London, England,

Manufactured in the United States of America.

Library of Congress Cataloging-in-Publication Data

Tracy, David.
    On naming the present : God, hermeneutics, and Church / David Tracy.
        p. cm.
    Includes bibliographical references and index.
    ISBM 0-88344-972-2 (paper)
    1. Modernism — Catholic Church. 2. Postmodernism — Religious aspects — Catholic Church. 3. Catholic Church — Doctrines — History — 20th century. 4. Theology — 20th century. I. Title.
BX1395.T72 1994
230'.2 — dc20

                                                                94-36878
                                                                CIP

ORBIS / ISBN 0-88344-972-2   SCM / ISBN 0-334-02588-5

Dedicated with great respect and affection
to
Paul Brand
whose wise guidance
Concilium has sought —
and received —
from its very founding

Contents

Part Five
Hermeneutical Issues and Theology

Preface

The chapters of *On Naming the Present* were all originally written as essays for the international theological journal *Concilium*. When my friend William Burrows of Orbis Books (the American publishers of *Concilium*) urged me to collect them in a single volume, as the first in a series of *Concilium* books that Orbis wished to publish, I readily agreed. My readiness was rooted in my firm commitment to the movement for continuing reform of church and society represented by *Concilium*.

The development of my own theology over time has been deeply influenced by my involvement in *Concilium* — as a member of the editorial board, as a writer, as an occasional editor of particular issues, and, above all, as a reader. Besides lifelong friendships established over the years with colleagues from Asia, Africa, Latin America, and Europe, I, as a North American theologian located principally in the secular academy, have been greatly aided by *Concilium* theology and its strong, often stern reminder that serious Christian theology must break out from both its academic and its First-World confinements to learn new ways to hear and be in genuine conversation with the most creative voices and thinkers in theology today — the theologies of an energizing world Christianity, the "two-thirds" worlds of Africa, Asia, Latin America, and Oceania, as well as the theological voices now powerfully speaking from Eastern and Central Europe since the end of the Cold War. Many academic theologians seem very reluctant to face how narrow their own perspectives may be and how contextual everyone's theology actually is. *Concilium* is one of the best cures for that crippling malady.

I felt some initial reluctance to collect my *Concilium* writings out of concern that, since each of the essays was written in the context of a topical issue of *Concilium*, they might prove too dependent on their original context to be interesting today. This fear proved real for four essays, which we have not reprinted here. The remaining essays were arranged not chronologically but topically for the purposes of greater readability and clarity. They will, I hope, introduce readers to some of the questions and concerns of the *Concilium* movement over the last twenty-odd years.

In rereading and editing the essays, I found myself, at several points, facing my own earlier theological self. At several points I wondered how I could have said *this* and, more often, why did I say it *that way?* Happily, that experience was infrequent enough (as I hope it will be to the reader) to allow me to move forward with the project as proposed. Therefore, I have altered essays as little as possible (usually, in fact, only for greater clarity) in order to remain faithful to the original context and content.

The editors at Orbis, in particular Kay Richardson, made several helpful suggestions for which I am very thankful. My writing, in not a few cases, has been rendered clearer than it was in the original thanks to their efforts. Substantively, however, the essays are the same as those originally published in the journal.

It was both interesting and instructive for me to re-encounter concerns and even occasionally parts and drafts of aspects of some of my published articles and books (especially, in earlier essays, *Blessed Rage for Order* and, then, chronologically *The Analogical Imagination, Plurality and Ambiguity,* and *Dialogue with the Other*), as well as aspects of my present major work-in-progress, *On Naming God.* At still other times, rereading the essays forced me to revisit issues and recall positions that I probably never would have faced without the urging of the editors of *Concilium.* Sometimes, indeed, a particular topic was not one I would "naturally," as it were, write about (for example, interpreting the Book of Exodus). In every instance, however, I eventually welcomed the challenge of having to think about and write about the assigned topic. It is good, at times, not to have the luxury of writing only on one's preferred issues but rather on an important and assigned issue. Happily, most of the topics were both assigned and personally preferred ones. Sometimes, the best essays (in my opinion) are on topics I had to think through "from scratch." I would very much like to return some day to several of those central theological issues. More importantly, I hope that readers of these essays (a genre that means, after all, "experiments" or "attempts") will try their own hand at raising the questions that *Concilium,* issue after issue, valiantly strives to articulate.

"*Concilium*" names as much the spirit of a movement for reform of church and society as it does a journal. Founded near the end of the Second Vatican Council by theologians deeply influential in that epoch-making Council — including Karl Rahner, Hans Küng, Yves Congar, Johann Baptist Metz, Edward Schillebeeckx and others), *Concilium* (published in German, Dutch, Portuguese, Spanish, Italian, French, and English) is designed to provide a bridge between the academic and pastoral worlds that marked the Second Vatican Council. *Concilium* has, I believe, remained faithful to that conciliar call to the spirit of reform of Vatican II even during recent years when that spirit has often seemed dormant in much of the official church — that is to say, at present, a time that can only be called a "restorationist period" in many ways. *Concilium* has also tried to be faithful to the equally needed reforms of culture, society, and academy by taking up, time after time, certain often neuralgic social, political, and cultural issues that more traditional and less pastorally oriented theological journals prefer to leave untouched.

I continue to believe that *Concilium* (both the journal and the wider movement of reform) provides the one genuinely international and ecumenical Roman Catholic voice that consistently risks articulating the kinds of theological rethinking needed for real reform. Inevitably in any such enterprise, sometimes the plans for reform will fail. More often, however, suggestions for reform are genuinely helpful for envisioning the kind of changes needed in an *ecclesia semper reformanda* as well as in a society, culture, and academy equally in need of continuing reform. In the amazingly pluralistic and complex Roman Catholic world, *Concilium* has clearly been one of the strongest voices that, in Jesse Jackson's elegant phrase, "keeps hope alive."

Perhaps the most important self-reform of *Concilium* over the last fifteen years lies in the shift of *Concilium* from its once Eurocentric theology to what can best be named not just a pluralistic but a polycentric theology. There are now many centers for genuine theological thought throughout the world. Those of us living in the North Atlantic and academic centers seriously impoverish ourselves and our theologies by ignoring (in what seems more and more like willful ignorance) this central fact of polycentrism in our really new theological situation. My own attempt to articulate that shift from Eurocentrism to polycentrism may be found in the first essay of this volume entitled "On Naming the Present." I hope that any North American reader who disagrees with my position on the need for a new, international, polycentric, dialogical theology will risk forging her or his own version of our common need. Surely the present reality of many centers of theology demands that each of us, wherever we are otherwise located, must learn better ways to hear again and respond critically to all the significant voices of other and different theologies.

The new prophetic call to a dialogical and polycentric theology is well represented, in the case of *Concilium*, by the frequently used *Concilium* phrase, the "mystical-political" dimension of Christian faith. This mystical-political emphasis has helped clarify two necessary theological moves which *Concilium* has tried to address. First, in a new kind of prophetic negative theology," *Concilium* has, in effect, insisted on the need for a new theological hermeneutics of suspicion, even a new kind of *via negativa* — a theological naming of the existing idols of church, society, culture, and academy. To name our contemporary idols is often the first step demanded by a serious theological assessment of our complex and troubling situation. Second, *Concilium* has also focused on the many situations of global suffering manifested by every clarification of the idols of our day. Thereby, a theologian may also develop a positive theological hermeneutics guided by the strength and, above all, the hope present in the struggles for justice and integrity across the globe. These two often intertwined moves — so powerful in the new theologies around the globe, so necessary in all serious theology wherever located — are fully representative of *Concilium* as both a journal and a movement at its best. This mystical-political emphasis suggests how the reforming movements released by Vatican II might have developed even in the official church structures if those movements had been left to their own self-critical dynamism (which, unfortunately, in many cases they were not).

Some of my own attempts to listen to the global ecumenical theological conversation represented by *Concilium* and to respond theologically to that conversation may be found in the essays that follow. Each of these essays, by its new life in the new context of this book, finds itself torn from its original place as an assigned essay on an assigned topic in the midst of other essays on the same topic in a carefully designed issue of the journal. By their new placing and life in this new context, the present essays will suffer some the inevitable loss of their original implicit conversation with the other essays on a topical issue of the journal. At the same time the essays in this new context of a book may now take on a new life and enter a new conversation with any reader of this book. I hope the essays will thereby encourage readers to join in larger global theological conversation of which these essays — as the *Concilium* movement as a whole — is a part. Perhaps some readers will even be encouraged to read the original issue of *Concilium* where the essay was born. Inevitably, there is some duplication of themes and positions here. But editors and other readers have assured me that in choosing these essays and eliminating others from those I have written for *Concilium* over the years, the final product works. The present essays bear the kinds of coherence of content, and (thanks to the demands of the various *Concilium* editors of the issues of which they were once a part) the kind of seriousness of purpose needed for any essay to merit a second life as a book.

I wish to thank, above all, William Burrows — friend of many years, once a student at the University of Chicago, and now managing editor at Orbis Books. Bill conceived this project, persuaded me to undertake it, saw it through to completion and advised me wisely, generously, and patiently all along.

I also wish to thank all my colleagues at *Concilium*. Among them, I single out the incomparable Dutch editor and my friend Paul Brand of Amsterdam to whom I dedicate this book. Paul, one of the founders of the journal, is a man whose commitment, critical sense, and graciousness represent *Concilium* at its best. *Ad multos annos!*

Chicago, 1994

Part One

On Naming the Present

1

On Naming the Present

I. Introduction: The Present and the Self

We live in an age that cannot name itself. For some, we are still in the age of modernity and the triumph of the bourgeois subject. For others, we are in a time of the leveling of all traditions and await the return of the repressed traditional and communal subject. For yet others, we are in a postmodern moment where the death of the subject is now upon us as the last receding wave of the death of God.

These three conflicting namings of the present situation are at the heart of the conflict of interpretations in that place which was once construed as the center of history — Western, including Western Christian theological, culture. But as its own conflict on how to name itself shows, that Western center cannot hold. For *modernity*, the present is more of the same — the same evolutionary history of the triumph and taken-for-granted superiority of Western scientific, technological, pluralistic and democratic Enlightenment. For *antimodernity*, the present is a "time of troubles" — a time when all traditions are being destroyed by the inexorable force of that same modernity. For the antimoderns, ours is a time to retreat to a past that never was and a tradition whose presumed purity belies the very meaning of tradition as concrete and ambiguous history. For *postmodernity*, modernity and tradition alike are now exposed as self-deceiving exercises attempting to ground what cannot be grounded: a secure foundation for all knowledge and life. For the postmoderns at their best, the hope of the present is in the reality of

Source: *Concilium* 1990/1, *On the Threshold of the Third Millenium*, edited by the Foundation on the occasion of *Concilium*'s twenty-fifth anniversary.

otherness and difference — the otherness alive in the marginalized groups of modernity and tradition alike — the mystics, the dissenters, the avant-garde artists, the mad, the hysterical. The conscience of postmodernity, often implicit rather than explicit, lives more in those groups than in the elite intellectual classes constituting their ranks.

For anyone in this troubled, quarreling center of privilege and power (and as a white, male, middle-class, American, Catholic professor and priest I cannot pretend to be elsewhere) our deepest need, as philosophy and theology in our period show, is the drive to face otherness and difference. Those others must include all the subjugated others within Western European and North American culture, the others outside that culture, especially the poor and the oppressed now speaking clearly and forcefully, the terrifying otherness lurking in our own psyches and cultures, the other great religions and civilizations, the differences disseminating in all the words and structures of our own Indo-European languages.

But even this turn to the other and the different by the modern West is too often made with the secret wish that we are still the center and can name those others. The others remain at the margins. Marginal from where? From the center which no longer holds. In theological studies, this naming continues, for example, when we not so innocently refer to "Near Eastern" and "Far Eastern" studies; near to whom? Far from what? The other envisaged from the self-named center is too often a projected other: one projected either by the new fears of the loss of privilege and power of the modern bourgeois subject, or the hopes for another chance of the neoconservative, or the desires for escape from modernity of the postmodern nonself. A fact seldom admitted by the moderns, the antimoderns, and the postmoderns alike — even with all the talk of otherness and difference — is that there is no longer *a* center with margins. There are many centers. Pluralism is an honorable but sometimes a too easy way of admitting this fact. Too many forms of modern Western theological pluralism are historicist, but too ahistorical as well as curiously a-theological in their visions to allow for the unsettling reality of our polycentric present. There is a price to be paid for any genuine pluralism — that price many pluralists seem finally either unwilling to pay or unable to see. It is that there is no longer a center. There are many. And the conflicts about how to interpret the Western present (modern, antimodern, postmodern) can often prove to be either blunt or subtle refusals to face the *fascinans et tremendum* actuality of our polycentric present. The others must become genuine others for us — not projections of our fears and desires. The others are not marginal to our centers but centers of their own. Their conflicts and their liberationist self-namings demand the serious attention of our center on their own terms.

If mere anarchy is not to be loosed upon the world without a center, then the polycentrism of our present situation must be faced. But how? Each of us can only face it from where we are. That "where" may demand a willingness at times to betray one's class, race, sex, or profession. That "where" surely demands an attempt to listen to others as other, coming to teach us new ways to read both gospel and situation. As Catholic Christians we are blessed to be part of a two-thousand-year-old tradition that was profoundly pluralistic from the very beginning (there are four gospels, not one) for all whose eyes are not blinded by a monolithic vision. We are blessed to live in a church that is ceasing to be a merely Eurocentric church and struggling to become a polycentric, a truly world church. We are also blessed to live in a period where the other great religious traditions — both the other Christian churches, the Jewish traditions, a resurgent Islamic tradition, the profound and polycentric Buddhist, Hindu, neo-Confucian, Taoist traditions, and all the great indigenous traditions throughout the world can finally be heard by us and learned from as genuine others, if we will it.

This series of blessings can seem an affliction — as the ancient Chinese curse suggests by stating "May you live in interesting times." But the aim of Christian theology — that nearly impossible, that always inadequate mode of thought and action — is to write the history of the present in the light of the gospel of Jesus Christ. To seize the heart of the matter of the Christian gospel in our present moment is to expose the false visions of the present which afflict us. Fortunately, none of us is alone in this effort. We find, rather, the emergence of a mystical-prophetic option emerging in myriad theological forms in all the centers of our polycentric church,[1] in the churches of Latin America, Asia, and Africa; in the movements for social and individual emancipation in the centers of Eastern and Central Europe; in the feminist theologies throughout the world; in the African-American and Native American theologies of North America; in the rethinking of the indigenous traditions of South and Central America. We always live in a time of danger — as the repressed histories of the oppressed in every culture show, as the memory of the cross and resurrection of Jesus Christ insistently brings to the attention of every

Christian generation. Only by facing the present danger with the memory of that passion and resurrection, with hope in the God who gave promises to overcome oppression, alienation, guilt, and death itself, can we learn together to name the present by joining in conversation and solidarity with the historical struggles of all the centers in a polycentric world and church.

Otherwise theology, even good theology, is in danger of becoming more consumer goods for an increasingly empty time and an ecologically devastated space. As Saul Bellow observes, the visions of genius always seem to become the canned goods of the intellectuals. So it is even with theology: where the vision of Thomas Aquinas could become the platitudes of the neo-Scholastics; where Karl Rahner's profound mystical envisagement of ordinary Christian life can be read as a belief in merely private experiences for a tired world; where the marginalized voice of the great mystics can become more consumer items labeled "peak experiences"; where the words and actions of the prophets can become mere ideology; where the ecclesial self-reforming impulses of Vatican II can become merely the embourgeoisement of Catholic Christianity.

"The real exile of Israel in Egypt was that they had learned to endure it,"[2] insisted Martin Buber. It is also our exile. We can justly pride ourselves, for example, on the power of modern communications but then fail to acknowledge technology's profound ambiguity. On the one hand, modern communications can cross all boundaries, disrupt totalitarian and authoritarian systems alike, and subvert all political, cultural, and ecclesial hegemonies. On the other hand, modern communications can also cross all borders only to level all traditions, subvert all communities, disempower all memory of suffering.

What tradition can withstand that power — a subtle, eroding, pervasive power to make all life banal, to empty all time, to remove all difference and otherness? The strange embrace of modern science, technology, and industrialism throughout the world has helped to render the present time for many an empty time — bereft of memory, free of hope, powerless to resist. The consumerism of our age is a relentless attack on the soul of every individual and every tradition.

In a present emptied of authentic time, the prophecy of H. Richard Niebuhr becomes disturbingly true: modern Western Christians may find ourselves preaching that "A God without wrath brought [humans] without sin into a Kingdom without judgment through the ministrations of Christ without a Cross."[3]

II. On Naming the Present — Modernity

The debates on the nature of modernity continue without end. Much of the debate is focused on the relationship of rationality and modernity. In Jürgen Habermas's case this discussion is a fruitful one. For without linking the many debates on rationality to a historical and social theory of modernity, debates on reason (including theological ones on the relationship of "faith" and "reason") tend very quickly to become ahistorical and purely formal. Since Hegel, it is clear that the fact that reason has a history is a problem for reason. How problematic, the contemporary discussions of rationality show by disclosing forms of pure relativism and historicism which live on the illusory hope that, by such intellectual retreats, we can at last take history and the limits of reason seriously. Awaiting the collapse of such historicized notions of reason is the last modern defender of ahistorical reason: positivism.

Positivism is intellectually a spent force — even in the natural sciences since the emergence of various forms of postmodern science (like ecological science) and in most post-Kuhnian forms of philosophy of science. But positivism is culturally as powerful a force as ever. Where positivism reigns, history is emptied of real time and becomes at best a bad infinity: an infinity of more of the same. The sameness is clear: only science (understood positivistically) can count for inquiry; reason is reduced to a purely technical function; technology continues with neither direction nor hope as its genuine liberating possibilities are mixed, without reflection, into a dominating and leveling power over all.

In the positivist view, whatever can be done technologically should be done. There is, for the modern positivist (whose numbers are legion), no reasonable way to discuss the good life, the call to happiness, the need for meaning in history and time. Like the ancient Roman empire, the new positivist technological culture makes a desert and calls it peace. That peace is clearly not the peace that comes with the prophetic call to justice. It is the peace of the sleepwalker and the justice of the bureaucrat.

The earlier great liberals — like William James with his generous call to a radical pluralism, like John Dewey with his persuasive account of the democratic ethos implied in non-positivistically construed scientific inquiry — now seem as helpless in the face of a reigning technocracy as are their neoconservative opponents. To be sure, the recent intellectual alliances in Europe and North America between a revised pragmatism and a revised hermeneutics offer a genuine hope for reason. But even that hope can be made a hope of reason alone — a reason not related to the social realities of a dominant scientific and technocratic culture.

Modernity, in sum, has become that which it most opposed and feared — one more tradition. The honest desperation of many modern secular thinkers reveals the pathos of liberalism in our period: the forces for emancipation set loose by the Enlightenment and the great modern revolutions may end trapped in a purely technical notion of reason from which there seems no honorable exit. No exit and no ethics. Above all, no genuine politics. This incredible century, which opened with a trust in science, reason, enlightenment, and modernity, finds itself facing at its end all that it thought it had long since buried: above all the resurgence of fundamentalist religions in their most aggressive forms. Modernity never opposed religion as long as it remained private and quietly hid away. Modernity never opposed art as long as it remained marginal as a distracting pleasure for the overworked bourgeois subject. But modernity did not expect and could not anticipate that even reason might one day yield its communicative, emancipatory role to a merely technical reason in a culture increasingly dominated by techno-economic concerns.

What hope, then, can there be for a public realm — that realm where all reasonable persons may enter to discuss the meaning and hopes for the good life, for happiness, for history and society — if only means but never ends can bear rational discussion? The classical political questions of happiness, the good life, the meaning of history have become as privatized and therefore as nonrational in essence as the classical questions of religion and art. It is little wonder that Max Weber could declare our situation an "iron cage" or Henry Miller could look at his culture and name it our "air-conditioned nightmare."

I admit to sharing much of this Weberian pessimism on our situation. But, finally, such pessimism is too total and unreal. Indeed, that total pessimism seems nothing less than the reverse side of the same coin of an earlier modern belief in progress. That myth of progress even survives, in more modest forms, in the taken-for-granted social evolutionary schemata of even such fine defenders of modernity as Habermas and Kohlberg.

The truth, indeed (as earlier secularization theologies were not wrong to argue) the theological truth of modernity still needs defense, including theological defense. For beyond a discredited myth of progress and against a wholesale Weberian pessimism lie the modern truths which Habermas and many other moderns have striven to defend: the reality of reason as communicative; the hopes alive in all the new countermovements to a dominant techno-economic realm; the drive to a Jamesian cultural pluralism and a genuine political democracy undivorced from economic democracy. The liberating power of all that is occurring in Eastern and Central Europe and elsewhere shows the power of that drive to modern democracy and pluralism. However, despite the portrait of these epoch-making events in much of the Western media and despite the self-congratulating claims of too many Western political and intellectual leaders, the hopes expressed in these great awakenings are not and do not wish to become carbon copies of Western modernity. As Vaclav Havel makes clear, it is not the techno-economic political culture of the West with its consumerism, possessive individualism, and hedonism which is his hope.

We are not trapped in Weber's "iron cage." But we have seen our lifeworlds, in all their rich difference, increasingly colonized by the forces of a techno-economic social system that does not hesitate to use its power to level all memory, all resistance, all difference, and all hope. Religion becomes privatized. Art becomes marginalized. All the great classics of our and every culture become more consumer goods for a bored and anxious elite. Even the public realm — the last true hope of reason in its modern and classical Western forms — becomes merely technicized. I do not hesitate to admire an enterprise like Habermas's noble modern defense of communicative reason united to his lucid and balanced account of the relationship of social action and social system in modernity. But until the social-evolutionary schema also informing Habermas's effort is exposed and challenged from within, until the claims to truth of art and religion are taken far more seriously, I cannot see how even that proposal can heal modernity.[4]

Modern theologies can also participate in a not-so-secret belief in Western social evolution. They fail thereby to see how impoverished the notion of reason has become in our techno-economic culture. To be sure, liberal theologies have faced with an unmatched honesty some of the dilemmas of the individual in our and every culture: the question of finitude; the realities of guilt and anxiety; the lingering power of meaninglessness in an empty time; a true consolation, in grief and mourning, in the face of death. But where, in all these modern theologies, is the acknowledgment that the techno-economic realm of modernity may quietly transform these religious realities into merely new consumer goods as readily as the systemic demands of the techno-economic realm have tried to turn modern reason into a merely technical reason?

The hope of reason must be defended in any philosophy worthy of the name. The great human questions of finitude, guilt, anxiety, and death must be clarified in any theology worthy of the name. But that hope and even those questions — in this modern situation — can only live if they become explicitly historical and political. In our theological context, the questions must become mystical-political. There is no more need to disparage the great liberal theologies than there is need to disown the achievements of the Enlightenment itself. The intentions of the liberal theologians were noble. Their accomplishments are real and retrievable, especially in the personal realm. But can personalism conquer in a culture ridden with possessive individualism? Can Christian hope be reduced to the ahistorical individual of modernity? Can reason be understood outside its historical, cultural, and social context? Can resistance be active if the empty time of modernity relentlessly invades all consciousness to render all consolation merely private?

One need not join the totalitarian critics of this modern society — whether Weberian or neo-Durkheimian or some forms of neo-Marxism. One need not join the wholesale attack upon the Enlightenment and modernity of neoconservatives and postmoderns alike. One need not engage in that curious form of self-hatred which some modern middle-class intellectuals, including theologians, seem at times to find so compelling. Considering the alternatives (including the alternatives of intellectual mystification and social and intellectual oppression against which the great middle-class revolutions honorably fought), an endangered democratic ethos, the classic middle-class virtues, and the pluralism of our modern societies deserve defense. They deserve theological defense at a time — our time — when all those accomplishments of the modern, bourgeois revolutions are in danger of destruction by a techno-economic realm out of control. This is especially the case in a church — our church — where even the genuine gains of modernity first released by Vatican II after two centuries of Catholic resistance to modernity are now stymied at every point by those whose views are not post-Enlightenment at all but, at best, pre-Enlightenment.

But what we also need to affirm is that none of the models of the modern self and the present time of modernity can any longer suffice: neither the purely autonomous self of the Enlightenment, nor the expressionist self of the Romantics, nor the anxious self of the existentialists, nor the transcendental self of the transcendental philosophies and theologies of consciousness. All such models are inadequate: for all are too deeply related to the embattled and self-deluding self of modernity. We need a new theological understanding of both self and the present time again. We need historical subjects with memory, hope, and resistance.

There are two major candidates in our period for a replacement of the modern individual and the empty time enforced by the reign of the techno-economic realm and its social evolutionary views. The antimodern communal self of the neoconservatives and the postmodern claim to nonselfhood and nonpresence. What hopes do they bring? What resistance do they offer?

III. On Naming the Present: Antimodernity in the Fundamentalists and the Neoconservatives

The first response of antimodernity may be called fundamentalism, a word that originated in Protestant controversies but that now covers a wide spectrum indeed: from the Islamic fundamentalism of Ayattolah Khomeini's movement to the Roman Catholic traditionalism of Archbishop Lefebvre's movement; from Rabbi Kehane's re-reading of Judaism, to the emergent Hindu fundamentalism in India and Shinto fundamentalism in Japan, and several of the new religious cults. What was least expected by modern Western liberal culture has happened: a resurgence of antimodern, antiliberal, antiprivatized, aggressive religious movements across the globe.

Religion, on the subconscious evolutionary schema of modernity, was supposed to pass away quietly — into the private recesses of consolation and nostalgia and into the enervated hopes of the emerging middle-class subject. But the vacuum left by modernity's leveling of all traditions led finally to an explosion of a resurgence of religion in its most traditionalist, premodern forms. As Walter Benjamin insisted in his time, it is a mark of the ahistorical historicism of modernity to think: "How can this happen in modern (i.e., enlightened) times?" The more reasonable question is how could this not happen in a time where there is no true time and to subjects deprived of their

traditions of memory and hope? Human beings cannot but ask the
limit-questions that religious traditions pose and respond to. The human demand for personal and historical meaning will not so easily be
pushed aside.

The fierce antimodernity of the Islamic revolution in Iran, like the
violent antisecularity of North American fundamentalists and the an-
tiliberationist violence of many Latin American fundamentalist
groups, bespeak a common message: the modern age has failed. An
explosion of fundamentalist movements throughout the globe is
upon us. Perhaps it is more accurate to name this phenomenon not
an explosion but an implosion. For fundamentalist groups (from the
electronic churches of the United States to the technologically sophisticated revolution in Iran through the use of modern media by
fundamentalist groups in Latin America) betray a common theme: all
the ethical and political values of modernity (individual rights, pluralism, a democratic ethos, a trust in public reason) must be rejected at
the very same time as modern technologized science and industrialism are embraced.

A strange fate indeed: the products of modernity are embraced by
fundamentalists while all the authentic values of the modern experiment are rejected. This rejection includes all theology which employs
modern scientific methods (like historical criticism and ideology critique) to rethink our troubled heritage. The very violence of the fundamentalist rejection of modernity illuminates the desperation of
human subjects sensing their loss of all community, tradition, and
values as they feel the terror of a history become empty and mean-
ingless. It is foolish to hope that fundamentalism will simply go away.
It is as close as the nearest television set. The power of fundamentalism in our day should teach the rest of us at least this much: on the
one hand, the human demand for historical significance and personal meaning will not be put off as easily as modernity, with its
deadening social-evolutionary teleology, assumed; on the other
hand, there are values in the modern experiment which all non-fun-
damentalists should deliberately defend: the value of the rights of the
individual, the freedoms of press, religion, assembly, and repre-
sentation won by the great bourgeois revolutions; the affirmation of
scientific inquiry without scientism; the demand to reflect critically
on technology rather than mindlessly embracing it; the affirmation of
pluralism and dialogue; the defense of a public realm; a trust in
democratic processes. No one of these modern values is without a
price. How high a price, the fundamentalist resurgence — with its

divorce from these modern and Christian values and its marriage with technology, industrialism, and scientism — disturbingly demonstrates.[5]

It must be frankly, even bluntly, stated that religious fundamentalism cannot be taken as an intellectually serious theological option any more than secular positivism, which it so resembles, is a serious philosophical option. But religious fundamentalism's social and historical power — again like positivism — is real and is growing. Its significance as a movement of troubled human beings and communities is a phenomenon that merits respect and theological attention from all. The non-fundamentalist version of antimodernity, on the other hand, merits not merely human but full intellectual respect. For here — as in conservative evangelical but not fundamentalist Christians in the Americas, as in Roman Catholic traditional theologies as distinct from the traditionalism of Lefebvre, as in the great resurgence of Islamic thought as distinct from Khomeini, as in the retrieval of Jewish traditions across all the forms of Judaism — the neoconservative revival is a profound and, in many ways, a heartening phenomenon.

For the neoconservative sees through the emptiness of the present and the poverty of the modern subject. The neoconservative knows that a present without past memory and tradition is self-illusory and finally self-destructive. The neoconservative knows that a subject without community and tradition is very soon little else than the modern possessive individual rendered passive and historyless. The neoconservative sees the folly of the Enlightenment's wholesale attack on the very concept of tradition. She or he senses the unreality of the assumed universalism in Western liberal social-evolutionary schemas applied to history. The neoconservative notes the wasteful and complacent obstruction of the rich resources of the tradition. She or he knows the need to retrieve these resources anew in our parlous times if we are to maintain any truly Christian identity at all.

Thus the emergence, in modern theologies, of honorable "postliberal" options: like the new Barthianism of the Yale school[6]; the new sectarian insistence on pure witness of much Western Christian ethics; the insistence of so many Catholic theologians that perhaps, after all, Bonaventure rather than Thomas Aquinas is the proper model for Catholic theology. The gains of these new postliberal theologies are clear for all to see: the recovery of the need for the biblical narrative as forming the identity of Christians both individually and

communally in the new Protestant narrative theologies of Frei, Lindbeck, Hauerwas, and many others; the recovery of the importance of
the visible form for Catholic life and thought in the light of God's own
self disclosure in the divine-human form of the incarnation of Jesus
Christ in the great theology of retrieval of Hans Urs von Balthasar; the
insistence that modernity can occasion the erosion of all communal
and even personal Christian identity in the call to reaffirm Christian
identity in the Roman Catholic theology of Ratzinger.

I do not see how any one of us cannot learn from these neoconservative theologies of retrieval: of narrative, visible form, tradition,
community, and identity. This is the case even for those of us who
dispute the adequacy of the neoconservative position on both theological and cultural grounds. It is not merely the neoconservatives'
frequent refusal to admit the genuine achievements of modern theology which disturbs. Indeed, that refusal should disturb anyone still
able to distinguish the genuine values of modernity from its distortions. It is not merely the partiality in the reading of the classic theologians chosen for attention: the unrelieved pessimism of Ratzinger's
reading of Augustine; the brilliant but disturbingly partial character
of von Balthasar's reading of Bonaventure and Dante; the apolitical
reading of Karl Barth by the new Barthians; the untroubled use of the
traditional neo-Scholastic distinction of the "natural" and "super-
natural" realms in the secularly liberating and ecclesially stifling political theology of Pope John Paul II. All this is troubling enough. But
consider as well what may happen to the very resources which the
neoconservative theologians have done so much to recover: the defense of tradition and the past to understand how our present moment need not be a merely empty present; the need for a communal
and not individualist notion of the dignity of the human person; the
reality of Christian identity as Christian and not merely as an epiphe-
nomenon of modern emancipation; the need for memory and narrative to assure that identity. All these resources are themselves in grave
danger of destruction by the too partial retrievals of the neoconservatives.

For the memory of the Christian is, above all, the memory of the
passion and resurrection of Jesus Christ. It is that dangerous memory
(Metz) which is most dangerous for all those who presume to make
his memory their own. And that memory releases the theological
knowledge that there is no innocent tradition, no innocent classic, no
innocent reading. That memory releases the moral insistence that the
memory of the suffering of the oppressed — oppressed often by the

church which now claims them as its own — is the great Christian countermemory to all tales of triumph: both the social-evolutionary complacent narrative of modernity and the all too pure reading of the "tradition" by the neoconservatives. Is the Christian narrative Christendom or Christianity?

Christianity is always a memory that turns as fiercely against itself as against other pretensions to triumph. The great prophetic negations of all triumphalism released by the memory of Jesus of Nazareth render unreal, on inner-Christian grounds, any appeals to narrative, memory, tradition, identity that partake of either innocence or triumph. To defend tradition is to defend that disturbing and often self-judging prophetic memory. To become historically minded is to seize that memory for the present and to recall the past in that memory's subversive light. As Benjamin insisted, "Every great work of civilization is at the same time a work of barbarism." Any theology of retrieval that refuses to face that fact may end, despite its own clear and noble intentions, not defending the memory of the cross and resurrection of Jesus Christ and not truly remembering the God who both promises and judges, but remembering only a form of Christianity dangerously close to historical Christendom.

IV. Postmodernity and the Death of the Modern Subject

Postmodern thought has exposed two illusions of modernity: the unreality of the notion of presence in modernity's concept of present time and the unreality of the modern subject's self-understanding as grounded in itself.[7] Like all achievements, this postmodern one is not without its own ambiguities. In its most radical form, postmodern thinkers can describe themselves as providing a "hermeneutic of the death of God." In an age where human subjects are everywhere in danger, postmoderns choose rather to complete the narrative of the death of God by adding the "death of the subject." It is not a heartening scenario.

To expose the illusory belief in pure presence of much modern thought is no small achievement. For modern thought is always attempting to ground itself in itself. Modernity, since Descartes, longs to build for itself its own foundations in a consciousness deceptively pure and an identify deceptively secure. As the postmoderns make clear, however, the modern self, unfortunately for its foundationalist

pretensions, must also use language. And the very self-decon-
structing, nongrounding play of the signifiers in all language will assure that no signified — especially the great modern signified, the
modern subject — will ever find the pure identity, the clear and distinct self-presence it seeks or the totality it grasps at. That self-
grounding, self-present modern subject is dead: killed by its own pretensions to grounding all reality in itself. Thanks to the postmoderns,
that subject should be unmourned by all.

Through their singularly deconstructive gestures of reflection, the
postmoderns act. Their best postmodern acts are acts of resistance:
resistance to modernity's complacently humanist self-image; resistance to a concept of the present bearing only an illusion of pure
presence: resistance to an alinguistic and ahistorical consciousness;
resistance, above all, to what Foucault nicely names "more of the
same."

Like Foucault, many of the postmoderns strive to rewrite the "history of the present." At their best they write their histories in such a
manner that formerly forgotten, even repressed, others of the modern tradition — hysterics, the mad, mystics, dissenters, avant-garde
artists — are allowed to speak and disrupt any empty modern present. Otherness, difference, and excess become the alternatives to the
deadening sameness, the totalizing system, the false security of the
modern self-grounding subject. Nietzsche returns. But he comes now
not as the "old" existentialist Nietzsche of troubled humanists. He
comes as the new, radically rhetoricized Nietzsche who laughs at the
abyss of indeterminacy he exposes in the bourgeois self-portrait of
the modern self and the nonpresence of the modern present.

In its theological forms, postmodern thinkers help us all to recover
the great mystics, especially the radically apophatic tradition from
Pseudo-Dionysius through Eriugena to Eckhart. They can also help
open Christian theology in and through their postmodern rethinking
of the "Godhead beyond God" of Eckhart to a dialogue with the en-
lightening nothingness (*sunyata*) beyond nihilism of the great Buddhist traditions.

With some notable exceptions, however, the postmodern thinkers
feel free to deconstruct the history of past and present rather than
actualizing any concrete ethical-political hope. They wish to deconstruct the *status quo* in favor of the *fluxus quo*. And yet they cannot
without further reflection on the ethical-political import of their own
deconstructive exposures. There is an implied ethics of resistance in
postmodern thought. But that ethic is one that is present often

against the grain of postmodern reflections on the impossibility of any determinateness. How can resistance be secured without some agent — not, to be sure, the false self-grounding subject of modernity, but rather the responsible self of the great prophets? Emmanuel Levinas, that most severe, partly because so close, critic of the postmoderns, knows this secret flaw of postmodern thought.[8] He, like them, knows that a desire for totality is the concealed wish and death-dealing fate of modern reason. Levinas knows that the issue is the issue of otherness, not more of the same. But unlike many postmoderns, Levinas also knows that the issue must be ethical-political: the face of the genuine other should release us from all desire for totality and open us to a true sense of infinity. The face of the other should also open us to the Jewish rather than Greek realities constituting our culture. For the face of the other can open us to ethical responsibility and even to the call of the prophets to political and historical agency and action.

Postmodern feminist thought is often the conscience of postmodernity. When reading a thinker like Julia Kristeva, one finds the unmourned modern subject dead.[9] But one also finds the emergence of a new subject beyond the usual no-self of the postmoderns: the subject-in-process-on-trial. The metaphor of process here, for once, is not merely another expression of a quietly evolutionary consciousness of unending process. The metaphor is rather both the relational metaphor of process and a legal metaphor of process as trial. We are all subjects-in-process-on-trial now.

The modern middle-class self thinks itself alive in those forms of modern ego-psychology which promise release, but finally return the ego to accepting the *status quo*. At the same time, there is emerging — through all those others marginalized by the official stories of modern Western triumph — a reality beyond the illusions of the modern ego and beyond postmodern reflections on otherness: the voices and actions of concrete others. Those others, especially the poor and oppressed in all cultures, now speak, unlike the postmoderns, as historical subjects of both resistance and hope. They insist that the future as both promise and judgment must interrupt all presentness even beyond the postmodern exposures of the false sense of the presence of modernity.

We need the enabling reflections of the postmoderns to expose the unreality of the present and the death of the modern, self-grounding self in all its myriad forms. We need, above all, the ability of postmodern thought to allow the marginalized ones — especially the mystics

— to speak once again. For the postmoderns are correct: many modern understandings of God, both philosophical and theological, are renderings of a transcendental signified; many anthropologies, including theological ones, are disguised anthropocentric humanisms where the theocentric reality of Christian faith is quietly disowned. But the postmoderns too often offer an honorable resistance to such modern self-illusions only to inform their resistance with a hope that seems little more than what Alan Bloom called nihilism with a happy ending.

Some of the marginalized can reenter the theological conversation through the postmoderns' preference for excess. But how do they reenter? As historical subjects? As ethical-political agents? As disruptive of the empty present not only through irony, laughter, and excess in the abyss of indeterminacy, but through the determinate and interruptive hope of the memory of the suffering of the living and the dead?

V. Conclusion: Mystical-Prophetic Resistance and Hope

On this reading, therefore, the attempts of moderns, antimoderns, and postmoderns alike to name our present are not finally successful. For nowhere in all this conflict of interpretations among moderns, antimoderns, and postmoderns does a full Christian theological naming of the present as interruptive eschatological time before the living God occur. For that we must listen to other conversations, especially those of people in our own and other cultures who experience massive global suffering but have found new voices of their own and new historical actions to match those voices.[10] Part of what one can hear in the voices of these "others," I believe, is the healing and transformative message of the Christian gospel alive once again: a message neither modern, nor antimodern, nor postmodern; a message to and for historical subjects in the concrete struggles for justice against suffering and oppression and for total liberation; a message also for our own time — a time that needs not merely better reflections on otherness and difference but needs above all to learn to listen and learn from others.

In each center of Christian theology in our situation, therefore, the varied and conflicting namings of the present are both promising and threatening. They are promising by discerning the gospel values embedded in our present struggles. In modern progressive theologies, for example, certain central values of both the gospel and the modern experiment of emancipation are defended and expanded. Consider modern theology's noble defense of pluralism and an authentic public realm for discussing values, ends, and the good life found in public theologies like the statements of the United States and Canadian bishops on nuclear war and the economy. These public theologies partake of the call to hope and resistance in a modern period where the public realm is in danger of being fully technicized by the colonizing encroachments of the techno-economic realm. Consider, as well, the expansion of the modern concern for individual human rights and genuine pluralism in the progressive, modern attempts to continue the self-reforming impulses of Vatican II in an age of official ecclesial retrenchment and reaction. The need for an ecclesial public realm to discuss the real differences and the unity amidst those differences and conflicts was never more clear, never more difficult to achieve. The modern theological concern for human rights has expanded to a theologically plausible defense of the values expressed by the modern experiment: a democratic ethos, a genuine pluralism, a defense of the role of public reason in all theology.

These progressive theologies, rooted in both the gospel and the modern experiment, have expanded their concerns, moreover, into three crucial areas that demand the attention of the entire theological community: the demands for justice for women in society and church as envisaged and made real in emancipatory feminist theologies throughout the world; the increased sense of the need for a new theology of nature in a time of an ecological crisis released by science, technology, and industrialism and enforced by the mindless policies of the techno-economic realms in capitalist and socialist societies alike; the progressive opening of Christianity to the other great religious traditions in genuine theological interreligious dialogue led by such progressive theologians as Hans Küng and John Cobb. All those great movements of hope — Christian and modern — participate in and expand the emancipatory power of the modern traditions in Christian theologies.

The neoconservative theologians, moreover, remind everyone that there is no real Christian present unless there is a constant retrieval of the resources of tradition, community, narrative-identity, the incarnational and sacramental power of the visible forms of Christian life and faith, and the claims to truth in all the classics of religion and art. The classics are defended with persuasive power by the neoconservatives in a time when religion and art alike are privatized into harmless abstractions for an overworked bourgeois subject uneasily anxious of its fading power.

Meanwhile, the postmodern movements, alert to the falsity of all notions of pure presence grounded in the prevalent concepts of the modern subject, have exposed once and for all the illusory character of the hopeless hope of modernity. Postmodernity at its best releases the voices of subjugated knowledge: the voices of all those marginalized by the official story of modern triumph. The postmoderns may help us all recover those marginalized voices anew. Even the radical apophatic mystical tradition may now show a postmodern way beyond the death of the modern subject to a new subject-in-process-on-trial before the living Godhead-beyond-God. That would be a genuine postmodern hope beyond the more usual scenario of the death of the subject following the death of God.

But, finally, all these modern Western namings of the present remain too self-centered and narrow. They name only the dilemmas of the Western center. By so limiting the range of their attention and thereby their ability to listen, converse, and act, they may trap themselves anew within their own conversation alone at the very time when there is emerging a new polycentric world and a world church where the most concrete others — the poor and the oppressed — speak and act. For the Western center, however named — modern, antimodern, or postmodern — cannot and should not hold as the center. If it clings to its former senses of being the center, this center cannot heal itself. It must turn in conversation and solidarity to all the other centers with respect for its own heritage allied to an exposure, at long last, to other heritages. Otherwise, the moderns will be tempted quietly, even unconsciously, to retreat to social-evolutionary scenarios which secure modern centeredness at the price of illusion for self and destruction for others. They will be tempted to hear others only as projected others — projections of their present fears and anxieties, hopes and desires. Otherwise, the antimoderns, in their intellectual neoconservative form, will be tempted to retreat into a wholesale reaction that will sometimes leave their policies of restoration distinguishable in theory but not in practice from the policies of the fundamentalists. A retrospective utopia has as little to do with a true Christian eschatological sense of time, subject, and community as does the social-evolutionary sense of time of modernity. It is merely evolution-in-reverse.

Without the wider conversation with others, moreover, the postmoderns — proud and ironic in their centerlessness — will be tempted not to heal the breach they expose in Western modernity. Having killed the modern subject, they too must now face their own temptation to drag all reality into the laughing abyss of that center-less, subjectless, but very Western labyrinth. Despite their honest an-tihumanist rhetoric, the postmoderns are tempted to create merely a new Western humanism with a human face. But that face may prove too radically ironic to maintain resistance. And that resistance may be too distrustful of any determinate hope to maintain any responsi-ble ethical-political, much less prophetic and eschatological, agent.

Where, in all the discussions of otherness and difference of the postmoderns as well as the moderns and the antimoderns, are the poor and the oppressed? These are the concrete others whose differ-ence should make a difference. For through them the full and inter-ruptive memory of the gospel is alive again among us. In their pro-phetic speech and their liberating actions lies hope for the true time of the present before a judging and saving God. In their actions, his-torical subjects act and speak for all who have ears to hear.

All the more familiar Western namings of the present have much to teach and much to warn themselves against. Only when the West-ern conversation ceases merely to reflect on otherness and difference and notices, listens to, joins in conversation and solidarity with the concrete others and the different in all the other centers will a new historical subject in the Western center itself emerge after the death of the modern subject. Only when moderns cease to believe that, as heirs to the Western tradition, they alone know what reason, conver-sation, praxis mean will they be able to converse with and enter into solidarity with the genuine others who also have their own stories, traditions, and modes of reason and practice. Only when the anti-moderns realize that a retrieval of tradition, memory, identity, cannot become an occasion to assume that we already know that identity from a too innocent reading of the past will they be able to hear anew the memories of suffering, the countertraditions of the oppressed alive in our day. If Western Christians wish to move to a new reserva-tion of the spirit, no modern bureaucrat will stop them. Only their conscience, alive to the interruptive memory of the suffering and res-urrection of Jesus Christ, will halt that slide into a museum-like cen-teredness.

The prophetic voices of our present may be found best, as they were for the ancient prophets and for Jesus of Nazareth, in those peoples, those individuals, and those new centers most privileged to

God and still least heard in the contemporary Western conflict of interpretation on naming the present: the suffering and the oppressed. These others are various and, to be sure, often conflicting theologies of liberation in all the other centers of our polycentric moment: Latin America, Asia, Africa, Eastern and Central Europe, as well as in the too often ignored centers of our own culture — the African-American theologians, the Native American theologians, the communities of Christian feminist and womanist theologians throughout the world. All now speak in such manner that, in Gustavo Gutiérrez's elegant phrase, we "drink from our own wells." In a parched space and empty time, the conversation must remain critical. The response cannot be one of mere modern liberal guilt, but of Christian responsibility — capable of responding, critically when necessary, to the other as other and not as a projection of ourselves. The result could be a new solidarity in the struggle for the true time of justice and a communal, theological naming of the present in a polycentric world and a global church led by these new voices. Such hope, in the Babel of our present, can seem a mirage. But such hope, grounded in the Pentecost of the time of the Spirit alive in many centers, does promise liberation for all. To resist ourselves and our present may be the first sign of that hope. To trust God — the living, judging, promising God of the prophets, mystics, and Jesus the Christ — and to act on that trust is the surest sign of that hope. The mystics and prophets are alive in unexpected ways among us. A mystical-prophetic theology with many centers is being born throughout the globe.[11] Is it too much to ask for our Western Christian tradition, in self-respect and self-exposure, to join that new conversation and enact that new solidarity? The true present is the present of all historical subjects in all the centers in conversation and solidarity before the living God. The rest is whistling in the dark.

NOTES

1. On the centrality of the memory of suffering, see Walter Benjamin's "Theses on the Philosophy of History" in *Illuminations* (New York 1968). Both quotations from Benjamin cited in this paper may be found in those Theses; the best Christian theological development of these themes (to which my reflections are often indebted) may be found in the work of Johann Baptist Metz, *Zeit der Orden? Zur Mystik und Politik der Nachfolge* (Freiburg

1977); *Glaube in Geschichte und Gesellschaft. Studien zu einer praktischen Fundamentaltheologie* (Mainz 1977).

2. Martin Buber, *Tales of the Hasidim*, vol. 2 (New York 1970), p. 315.

3. H. Richard Niebuhr, *The Kingdom of God in America* (New York 1959), p. 193. I have taken the liberty in the quotation here to change Niebuhr's word "men" to [humans].

4. I defend my analysis, defense, and critique of Habermas on these issues in an essay on Habermas in a volume that includes his response, entitled *Critical Theory and Public Theology*, Don S. Browning and Francis Schüssler Fiorenza, eds. (New York 1991).

5. See the incisive essays on fundamentalism in *Fundamentalism Observed*, vol. 1, Martin E. Marty and R. Scott Appleby, eds. (Chicago 1991) and Langdon Gilkey's essay in *Morphologies of Faith: Essays in Religion and Culture in Honor of Nathan A. Scott, Jr.*, Mary Gerhart and Anthony Yu, eds. (Atlanta 1990).

6. The most helpful North American study here is William C. Placher, *Unapologetic Theology. A Christian Voice in a Pluralistic Conversation* (Louisville 1989).

7. For representative studies here see: Jonathan Culler, *On Deconstruction. Theory and Criticism after Structuralism* (Ithaca 1982); Allen Thiher, *Words in Reflection. Modern Language Theory and Postmodern Fiction* (Chicago 1984). For major participants in the debate, see Jurgen Habermas, *Der philosophische Diskurs der Moderne* (Frankfurt am Main 1985) and Jean-Francois Lyotard, *The Post-Modern Condition. A Report on Knowledge* (Minneapolis 1984). For three very different theological responses to postmodernity, see Joseph S. O'Leary, *Questioning Back. The Overcoming of Metaphysics in Christian Tradition* (New York 1985); Mark C. Taylor, *Erring: A Postmodern A/theology* (Chicago 1984); David Tracy, *Plurality and Ambiguity. Hermeneutics, Religion, Hope* (San Francisco/London 1987).

8. See especially Emmanuel Levinas, *Totality and Infinity: An Essay on Exteriority* (Pittsburgh 1980).

9. See Julia Kristeva, *Desire in Language* (New York 1980); *Powers of Horror* (New York 1980).

10. Of the many works here, see especially the now classic text of Gustavo Gutiérrez, *A Theology of Liberation* (Maryknoll/London[2] 1986); *We Drink from Our Own Wells: The Spiritual Journey of a People* (Maryknoll/London 1981); *On Job. God-Talk and the Suffering of the Innocent* (Maryknoll/London 1987). On feminist theology, see Anne Carr, *Transforming Grace: Christian Tradition and Women's Experience* (San Francisco 1988); Rosemary Radford Ruether, *Sexism and God-Talk. Toward a Feminist Theology* (Boston/London 1983); Elisabeth Schüssler Fiorenza, *In Memory of Her: A Feminist Theological Reconstruction of Christian Origins* (New York/London 1983).

11. See Claude Geffre and Gustavo Gutiérrez, eds., *The Mystical and Political Dimensions of Christian Faith, Concilium* 96 (Edinburgh 1974) as well as the development of this term in the ongoing work of Edward Schillebeeckx. Many issues of *Concilium* following this groundbreaking 1974 volume may be read as developing this mystical-political (or, as I prefer, mystical-prophetic) option.

Part Two

On God

2

The Paradox of the Many Faces
of God in Mono-Theism

I. Monotheism and Its Different Meanings

The first problem with monotheism is the word itself. Although its basic meaning is clear (*monos-theos*: the one-God) that meaning changes into a surprising multiplicity as the horizon for understanding the word "monotheism" shifts. Wittgenstein's insistence that meaning is not an abstract property of words but is discovered by noting the *use* of a word in a context is nowhere more true than in a case like the word "monotheism." It is the ever shifting contexts that change the meaning.

At least three contexts are worth noting here. First, "monotheism" is a modern philosophical word meaning an abstract property (oneness) that belongs to God alone. More exactly, "monotheism" is an Enlightenment invention (H. More, D. Hume) that bears all the marks of Enlightenment rationalism. Monotheism, in this not so secretly evolutionary view, is a contrast word to "polytheism," i.e. (by Enlightenment standards), monotheism is a more rational understanding of the logic of the divine as implying a unicity of divine power, not a dispersal of that power into many gods and goddesses. Like the other famous "isms" of the Enlightenment (deism, pantheism, theism, panentheism) modern philosophical "monotheism" is, above all, "rational" and "ethical." The relationship of this Enlightenment notion of monotheism to the historical religions (especially but

Source: *Concilium* 1995/2, *The Many Faces of the Divine*, edited by Herman Häring and Johann Baptist Metz.

not solely Judaism, Christianity, and Islam) is often obscured by Enlightenment prejudice against "positive" (i.e., historical) religions in
contrast to "natural religion." Unfortunately most philosophical and
even many theological uses of the word "monotheism" still bear this
dehistoricized and decontextualized Enlightenment meaning.

A second context also presents itself for understanding the word
monotheism — history of religions. In a history of religions context
"monotheism" is a category employed to describe the "family resem-
blances" among different religious phenomena: the "high gods" of
some primal traditions (e.g., the *deus otiosus* traditions in Africa); the
philosophical reflections of the logic of unicity among the Greek
thinkers from Xenophanes to Aristotle; a possible name for some In-
dian thinkers (especially Ramanujan); a clear name for such religions
as Sikhism and Zoroastrianism; the revisionary monotheism of the
reforming Pharaoh Akhenaton; above all, of course, the three classical "religions of the book" or, in history of religions terms, the historical, ethical, prophetic monotheism of Judaism, Christianity, and
Islam. Clearly such history of religions' reflections have influenced
modern scholarship on the history of ancient Israel as well as the
history of early Islam. Many scholarly studies show the final emergence of radical monotheism in the "Yahweh alone" prophets (especially Amos, Elijah, and Hosea). This movement culminated in the
prophet of the Babylonian exile (Deutero-Isaiah). There Yahweh is
clearly not only the God of Israel but also both creator of the whole
world and the one and only God who determines not only Israel's
history but all history: recall Deutero-Isaiah's reading of the Persian
king Cyrus as the "Messiah" appointed by Yahweh. It is the Deuteronomic reading of Yahweh which will influence the theological — i.e.,
radical monotheistic — reading of Israel's history in the Bible. From
that point on, the central religious affirmation of Judaism, Christianity, and Islam will be the classic *schema Yisrael* of Deuteronomy 6:4-
5: "Hear, O Israel: The Lord our God is one Lord; and you shall love
the Lord your God with all your heart, and with all your soul, and with
all your might!"

The route to this radical monotheism, however, was a long and
complex one whose many twists and turns are still debated among
scholars. Indeed, there are few more fascinating debates in the history of religion than the conflict of interpretations among scholars of
ancient Israel on the most likely history of the emergence of radical
monotheism from polytheism, henotheism, monarchic monotheism,
and monolatry. There can be little doubt that, in the emergence of

radical monotheism in ancient Israel, there have been as many forms for the divine reality as there were names for the divine power(s). In strictly historical terms, radical monotheism is a relatively late arrival in the founding history of ancient Israel. But the principal theological question of today for Jews, Christians, and Muslims is not so much the theological implications of the fascinating history of the earlier different names and forms for the divine in the complex history of ancient Israel, but rather the still contemporary theological question of the different *forms* for the experiencing, naming, and understanding of divine reality since the prophetic and Deuteronomic emergence of radical monotheism.

Hence, the third, and for present purposes, the principal context for understanding the word monotheism is the strictly theological context of the category for monotheistic Judaism, Christianity, and Islam. For the purpose of clarity, this theological–soteriological understanding of historical ethical monotheism bears the following characteristics:

(1) God is one: an individual distinct from all the rest of reality.
(2) God is the origin, sustainer, and end of all reality.
(3) God, therefore, is the One with the person-like characteristics of individuality, intelligence, and love.
(4) God, and God alone, is related to all reality. Indeed God is Creator of all reality both natural and historical.
(5) In sum, God alone, as the Wholly Other One, is both transcendent to all reality and totally immanent in all reality.
(6) God discloses God-self in chosen prophets, historical events, and scriptures.

II. Islamic and Jewish Monotheism and the Many Faces of God

Among the three historical radically monotheistic religions, Islam has been the most insistent on the centrality of the oneness of God. The monotheism of Islam is not only a soteriological monotheism but a profoundly dogmatic one. Indeed, the dogma of the oneness of God (*tawhid*) is the central dogma of Islam. This absolute otherness of God is kept alive in every form of Islamic practice and thought. But this Islamic insistence on God's transcendence is never to be misinterpreted (as unfortunately it still is by secular and even Christian thinkers) as implying the remoteness or distance of God from humankind. Indeed Islam's genius for keeping God's transcendent oneness (and thereby otherness) the central dogma in all Islamic life has provided a rich sense, not of remoteness, but of the closeness and presence of God in Islamic life and thought. Islam (precisely as a word meaning "surrender to God") has a great theological hermeneutics of suspicion upon all forms for representing Allah since any form might obscure God's total otherness and transcendence, i.e., God's oneness (*tawhid*). Of the three radically monotheistic religions, Islam is the most hesitant in encouraging different "faces" of the divine. Above all God's oneness must never be compromised. At the same time, as the great Islamic mystical traditions (especially, but not solely, the Sufis) as well as the sheer beauty of the stark forms of Islamic art and culture show, Islamic radical monotheism has its own ways — mystical, artistic, theological piety — to portray the many faces of the One God.

This openness to many forms of the divine is even more the case in the other two radically monotheistic religions, Judaism and Christianity. Indeed, probably the richest theological discussion today of radical monotheism is the extraordinary debate in Jewish thought. Consider the great range of modern and postmodern Jewish options here: the insistence from Moses Mendelssohn to Herman Cohen and many contemporary thinkers in the Reform tradition that Judaism is quintessentially "ethical monotheism"; the complex existential categories for divisions within God occasioned by God's relationship to human suffering in F. Rosenzweig; the reflections of both God's "absence" and God's presence in every I–Thou relationship in M. Buber; the great recovery of the many diverse faces of the one God in the mystical, especially kabbalistic, traditions of Judaism recovered by G. Scholem through M. Idel and so many other contemporary scholars; the new post-Shoah "mad midrash" reflections on the faces of God (E. Fackenheim and E. Wiesel); and the new covenantal orthodox Jewish theologies on the disclosures of God in history (D. Hartman). One cannot but be struck by the amazing vitality, proliferation, and intense conflict of interpretation on how to interpret Judaism's profoundly monotheistic understanding of God. To summarize some of the most important aspects of this great monotheistic tradition: from the classical Jewish insistence never to name G_d, through the debates (at once Rabbinic and modern philosophical) on Jewish "ethical monotheism," through F. Rosenzweig's reflections on the *schema Yisrael* and *shekinah* that takes place within God as God gives God-self to the people Israel, to the intensely mystical and daringly speculative understandings of the very material letters of God's names in the Kabbalah, therefore, the question of the many faces of the one God has returned with explosive and creative force in contemporary Judaism.

In Judaism, Christianity, and Islam, monotheism is a religious before it is a philosophical category. Indeed, even within theology itself, soteriological monotheism is older than and grounding to all dogmatic monotheism. For the Jew, the Christian, and the Muslim monotheistic faith is fundamentally a gift of God: God's gift of self-revelation. Philosophical discussions of monotheism are indeed welcome and often relevant (e.g., for issues of credibility and intelligibility) in strictly theological analyses of religious monotheism. But for Jewish, Christian, and Muslim believers monotheism is fundamentally gift, grace, faith: *credere Deum Deo* — to believe in God through God's own self-revelation: in the covenant with the people Israel; in the Koran given to the prophet Mohammed; and in Jesus the Christ.

III. Christian Identity of God and the Many Faces of God

To understand the many faces of the divine in Christianity means to understand who God is in and through the revelatory event which is, for the Christian, the decisive mediation, as self-revelation, of God: the person of Jesus Christ. A Christian understanding of God becomes the question of the identity of God: who is God? For the Christian, God is the One who revealed God-self in the ministry and message, the cross and resurrection of Jesus Christ. A Christian theological understanding of God cannot ultimately be divorced from this revelation of God in Jesus Christ: neither through solely philosophical understandings of "monotheism" (although these philosophical arguments are, of course, relevant for questions of intelligibility); nor through historical-critical reconstructions, of "the historical Jesus" (although these reconstructions, even if never constitutive of Christian self-understanding, are relevant as corrections of traditional views — e.g., Docetic, Monophysite, and merely traditionalist christologies). The full Christian doctrine of God discloses the many faces of divine reality that must inform every symbol and doctrine just as the doctrine of God is informed in its many faces by every symbol and doctrine (creation-redemption, eschatology, church, spirit, sacrament, revelation and especially christology). A theological insis-

tence on the interconnection of the central mysteries of the faith is
true, of course, of the understanding of every great symbol of Christian faith, but is especially crucial on the question of God and the
many faces of the divine. Christian theology must always be radically
theocentric so that no single symbol or doctrine in the whole system
of doctrines can be adequately understood without explicitly relating
the symbol to the reality of God as disclosed in Jesus Christ.

The passion narratives, nicely described by H. Frei as "history-like"
and "realistic," disclose the most basic Christian understanding not
only of the identity of Jesus Christ but, in and through that identity,
the identity of the God who acts with the "face" of the Divine Agent in
and through the actions and sufferings of Jesus of Nazareth. As in any
realistic narrative, so, too, in the passion narrative an identity is rendered through the plotted interactions of an unsubstitutable character (Jesus) and the unique events (betrayal, cross, resurrection) which
Jesus both performs and suffers. The fact that the Christian understanding of the one God is grounded not in a general philosophical
theory of monotheism but in this concrete passion-narrative history
of God's self-disclosure as Agent in the cross and resurrection of Jesus
of Nazareth is the primary theological foundation of all properly
Christian understandings of God and the many faces of God.

The passion narrative, moreover, should not remain isolated from
the rest of the scriptures nor from the later creeds. Rather, the passion narrative, as foundation and focus of all properly Christian understanding of God, should open up to the larger gospel narratives on
the message and ministry of Jesus, the theologies of Paul and John,
the Pastorals, the Book of Revelation, and all the rest of the New
Testament. The many faces of God, for the Christian, are found,
therefore, not only in the foundational insight into God's "face" as
principal agent in the passion narratives and thereby in all history
and nature. God is also disclosed through the pre-passion actions of
the ministry and message of Jesus of Nazareth as they are rendered in
importantly different ways in the four gospels. The typical speech of
Jesus, for example, becomes part of the way through which Christians
understand the many faces of God: the parabolic discourse on the
Reign of God discloses God's face as an excess of both power and love
(e.g., the Prodigal Son); the typical word of Jesus for God, Abba, becomes crucial for any Christian understanding of the Power ("Lord")
and Mercy (Father) of the mysterious face of God disclosed through
Jesus; the centrality of the cross in the apocalyptic tale told by Mark
and the dialetical language of Paul also opens later Christians to the

tremendum et fascinans face of God disclosed in the hidden-revealed God of Luther, Calvin, and Pascal; the intrinsic link of Jesus' actions to the poor, the oppressed, and the marginal especially in Luke and Mark open many Christians to discovering the face of God above all in the faces of the victims of history and all those involved in the prophetic struggle against all oppression.

At the same time, as focused and grounded in the understanding of God's agency in the passion narrative, the Christian understanding of God should also open to the complex and profound disclosures of God's identity in the history of Israel rendered in the many genres (narrative, law, praise, lamentation, wisdom) of the Old Testament. This is clearly not the place to review and interpret the extraordinary complexity of a full scriptural understanding of the many faces of God disclosed in the many scriptural genres to name God. This much, however, does need to be affirmed: for the Christian, God is above all the One who disclosed the authentic face of God in raising Jesus of Israel from the dead. God, for the Christians, is the One who revealed decisively who God is in and through the message and ministry, the incarnation, cross, and resurrection of none other than Jesus the Christ. The most profound Christian metaphor for the true face of God remains the metaphor of First John: God is Love (1 John 4:16). To understand that metaphor (which occurs, let us note, in the first theological commentary on the most theological and meditative of the four gospels), is to understand, on inner-Christian terms, what has been revealed by God of God's very identity as agent and as the very face of Love in the ministry, the message, the incarnation, cross, and resurrection of Jesus Christ.

The answer to the question "who is God?" therefore, for the Christian faithful to the self-disclosure of God in Jesus Christ, is: God is love and Christians are those agents commanded and empowered by God to love. However, if this classic Johannine metaphor "God is love" is not grounded in and thereby interpreted by means of the harsh and demanding reality of the message and ministry, the cross and resurrection of this unsubstitutable Jesus who, as the Christ, discloses God's face turned to us as Love, then Christians may be tempted to sentimentalize the metaphor by reversing it into "Love is God." But this great reversal, on inner Christian terms, is hermeneutically impossible. "God is Love": this identity of God the Christian experiences in and through the history of God's actions and self-disclosure as the God who is Love in Jesus Christ, the parable and face of God.

To affirm that "God is love" is also to affirm, now, in the more abstract terms proper to postscriptural metaphysical theologies, that the radically monotheistic God, the origin, sustainer, and end of all reality, is characterized by the kind of relationality proper to that most relational of all categories, love. God, the One Christians trust, worship, and have loyalty to, can be construed, in more abstract terms, as the radically relational (and, therefore, personal) origin, sustainer, and end of all reality.

To affirm that the Christian understanding of God refers to the One whom Christians worship, trust, and are loyal to is also to "place" this Christian understanding on the language-map of radical monotheism (shared by Judaism and Islam). To affirm, with First John, in and through the gospel narrative and the ecclesial confession of the incarnation, cross, and resurrection of Jesus Christ, that "God is love" is further to affirm the radical relationality of God's nature as ultimately mysterious yet person-like (i.e., characterized by intelligence and love). The latter affirmation, moreover, both grounds a theological understanding of the economic Trinity in the primary Christian confession of Jesus Christ while also suggesting how the immanent Trinity can be understood in and through the economic Trinity. Christian monotheism is a Trinitarian monotheism. For the Trinitarian understanding of God is the fullest Christian theological understanding of the radical, relational, loving, kenotic God who revealed God-self in and through the incarnation, the ministry (healing, preaching, actions), the name "Abba" for God and the parables on "Reign of God," the fate of the cross and the vindication of the resurrection of Jesus of Nazareth and the disclosure of this Jesus as the Christ through the power and activity of the Spirit. It is impossible to separate theo-logy and Christology. In that same sense, the Christian understanding of the "existence" and "nature" of the radically monotheistic God must be grounded in the "identity" of the God disclosed in the many faces suggested by the history and effects of Jesus Christ. Each of the three classical radical monotheistic traditions finds its own route to the many faces of the one God. The Christian finds that route in and through the many faces of the one God disclosed decisively through the Spirit in Jesus Christ, the face of God.

BIBLIOGRAPHICAL INFORMATION

For further information and bibliography, see:

1. "Monotheism" article by Theodore M. Ludwig in *The Encyclopedia of Religion*, vol. 10, Mircea Eliade, editor-in-chief (New York 1957), 66-36.

2. H. Richard Niebuhr, *Radical Monotheism and Western Civilization* (New York 1960).

3. Bernard-Henri Lévy, *La Testament de Dieu* (Paris 1979).

4. Jürgen Moltmann, *The Trinity and the Kingdom: The Doctrine of God* (London 1981).

5. *Concilium*, vol. 177: *Monotheism*, Claude Geffré and Jean-Pierre Jossua, eds. (1985).

6. Hans Frei, *The Identity of Jesus Christ* (Philadelphia 1975).

3

The Return of God
in Contemporary Theology

I. Introduction: *Theos* and *Logos* in Theo-logia

The history of theology is the history of the ever-shifting relationship between the reality of God and that divine reality as experienced
and understood from within a *logos*, i.e., a particular horizon of intelligibility. The theologian is one who attempts the nearly impossible
task of correlating *theos* and *logos*. When that central responsibility is
poorly executed, the *logos* of some contemporary intelligibility over-
whelms and domesticates the reality of *theos*. Then theology — as in
the modern period — becomes obsessed with finding the exactly
right method, the irrefutable modern argument, the proper horizon
of intelligibility for comprehending and perhaps controlling God. To
be sure, insights continue to occur. Genuine arguments are forged.
Brilliant speculations ensue. Better methods, more exact and exact-
ing hermeneutics are developed. All the modern achievements of
theology are indeed significant. But we are all, willingly or unwill-
ingly, being forced to leave modernity. We leave it with genuine new
insights, thanks to the modern *logos*, into the reality of God. Modern
theology has forged an understanding of God understood as the
uniquely relational individual. For God — and God alone — is related
to all reality as the origin, sustainer, and end of all reality. And yet
many contemporary theologians who hold, as I do, that modern theology has indeed made a permanent contribution to the history of

Source: *Concilium* 1994/6, *Why Theology*, edited by Werner Jeanrond and
Claude Geffré.

theology by forging various and increasingly sophisticated relational concepts to understand God's radically relational nature better than premodern theologies did now hesitate to affirm that achievement without questioning. The awe-some, frightening, interruptive reality of God can seem lost even in the best modern concepts forged to articulate the relational insights of modern theologies.

Contemporary theology can be called by many names. None of those names suffices as the strange name "postmodernity" makes clear. But, at its best, postmodern theology is an honest if sometimes desperate attempt to let God as God be heard again; disrupting modern historical consciousness, unmasking the pretensions of modern rationality, demanding that attention be paid to all those others forgotten and marginalized by the modern project. *Theos* has returned to unsettle the dominance of the modern *logos*. There can be little doubt that in modern theo-logy, the *logos* of modern intelligibility was the dominant partner in the correlation. There can also be little doubt that across many forms of contemporary theology the power of God is once again the dominant partner in the theological correlation. A brief historical reflection on this development may aid our present assessments.

II. A Theonomous Question: Who Is God?

The question of God in the Scriptures is not primarily the question of the existence, nature, and attributes of God but the question who is God? For the Christian that question is answered decisively in and through the event and person of Jesus Christ. In Jesus Christ, the sacrament of God, Christians discover both who God is and who they are commanded and empowered to become. Christians learn the identity of God by learning the identity of Jesus as the Christ. This identity Christians learn principally through the history-like realistic passion narratives of the four gospels.[1]

Each of the four gospel narratives tells that story in a distinct, indeed different, way: from the strange apocalyptic tale of Mark, through the wisdom narrative of Matthew and the realistic hero's quest of Luke, to the meditative narrative of John and the disturbing, dialectical reflections on Christ Crucified of Paul. Yet each biblical telling also renders a single identity: the identity of God is disclosed in and through this unsubstitutable Jesus, the identity of Jesus is disclosed through his narrated words and actions, doings and sufferings, cross and resurrection. The first great Christian metaphor of God — God is Love (1 John 4:16) — occurs in the first letter-commentary on John's meditative gospel. As the gospel of John made clear through linking its theological meditations to the narrative of Jesus, the reality of God as Love can never be divorced, for the Christian, from the disclosure of God's reality and power in the narrated history of Israel, nor from God's wrath and suffering in Christ, nor from Jesus' lamentations toward God (My God my God, why have you forsaken me?), nor from Jesus' vindication as the Christ in the resurrection.

There is little wonder that the early Christian theologians could find Trinitarian language so fitting for their understanding of God — an understanding achieved in their liturgies and their lives by their experiences of God in the Spirit through the Word to the Father. It is also little wonder that Christian theologians, alive to the Greek horizon of intelligibility within which they lived and thought, could also find not only love but also intelligence so ready a clue to the nature of God whose identity they found decisively disclosed in the Word, Jesus Christ. Through the whole patristic and medieval periods, these two central realities — intelligence and love — became the principal clues for understanding the nature of the God identified as Love in Jesus Christ. Scholastic theology would nicely name a partial, incomplete, analogous but real understanding of the Ultimate Mystery who is God through reflections on both intelligence and love. Some theologians — Augustine and Aquinas prominent among them — would develop these brilliant analogies of intelligence and love to help Christians understand a little more of the nature of God. Rarely since those theonomous times have theologians managed to allow the reality of the God disclosed in Jesus Christ to function so well in their theologies. That divine reality was always illuminated but never controlled by the *logos* of Greek and Roman and medieval cultures on the nature of intelligence and love. Love as Greek *eros* was experienced and understood to be transformed by divine *agape* into Augustine's *caritas*. Human active intelligence was employed to provide some glimpse — however transitory — into a world of mathematical and dialectical intelligibility become an entry-point into the world of pure Divine intelligence.[2] It is refreshing even today to read the still startling achievements of the great patristic and medieval theologians on understanding the God of Jesus Christ by means of their transformation of the Greco-Latin *logos* on both love and intelligence. In some ways these earlier theonomous reflections on understanding God through understanding and transforming Greek love and intelligence are not merely permanent but unsurpassed and perhaps unsurpassable achievements. That remains the case at least until such time as theologians can glimpse again that earlier amazing and optimistic vision: the participatory understanding of all reality as sheer intelligibility and the whole cosmos as erotic. Only some forms of modern science — as Teilhard de Chardin saw — share that earlier optimism on reason and desire alike.

Even through the centuries dominated by these theonomous achievements of understanding God as Love and Intelligence, however, two alternative unsettling undercurrents were always at work. The first undercurrent challenged even the highest achievements of the theologians employing Greek understandings of intelligence for attempting a better understanding of God-self as Pure Intelligence. Again and again the refrain occurs above all in the great line from Dionysius the Areopagite through John Scotus Erigena through one side of Thomas Aquinas through Eckhart and Cusanus. The Incomprehensibility of God disclosed in and through God's very comprehensibility became an ever more radical testimony of increasing apophaticism. It functioned as a strong undercurrent become, finally, a powerful undertow to all theological confidence in the many uses of the *logos* of Greek intelligibility.

At the same time — now through apocalyptic movements and Pauline theologians of the cross — another and even more unsettling underground current drove much Western Christian theological reflection: the reality of God was revealed not in glory or *eros* or intelligence but in the hiddenness of the cross — i.e., God is revealed in the weakness, conflict, suffering of this Jesus Christ. All those Christians who could never forget the Hidden God disclosed in Mark's troubled narrative and reflected upon in Paul's unrelenting dialectic of the cross awaited the day when this great undercurrent would resurface. Then it would function not as a powerful and unsettling undertow to all intellectualist theologies of God (like the apophatic traditions on Divine Incomprehensibility did) but more like a flood that invaded and finally overtook the consciousness of many Christians. Surely this Pauline-Markan insight did resurface in the profound sense of the hidden-revealed God of Luther, Calvin, and Pascal. Here the new existential sense of *theos* as revealed in the hiddenness of the cross almost overwhelmed the *logos* of prior ages on love and intelligence. Indeed at times this existential experience of God's revelation only in hiddenness came close to overwhelming any cultural horizon of understanding at all. Hence all formal appeals to reason, to intelligence, to *eros* were often abandoned in favor of the radically Hidden God in Luther's brilliant and intense theological outbursts or Pascal's terror at the silence of infinite space at the very dawn of modernity. On the whole, however, as modernity took over, all these currents went underground again as the modern *logos* took over *theo-logia* and recast the understanding of God into properly modern terms.

III. God within the Modern Logos: From Deism to Panentheism

The Hidden God of Luther, so explosive in the Reformation, was transformed in early modernity into a profoundly anxious sense of the silence of infinite space in Pascal. Indeed Pascal is the quintessential early modern who, almost alone, saw both modernity's overpowering strength and its destructive power as eliminating the very sense of God's reality. The Godhead beyond God of Eckhart also went underground again after a last brilliant efflorescence in the most balanced of the great Renaissance thinkers, Nicholas of Cusa — the only theologian in whom the *logos* of mathematical intelligibility, the sense of infinity in early Renaissance modernity, and the apophatic tradition united into one last great outburst of a neo-Platonic, an oddly optimistic "*docta ignorantia.*" [3] In the meantime, the relentless progress of modernity took over all thought, including the thought of God.

The difficulty of modernity on the question of God can now be seen with clarity. So strong, so new, so powerful was the modern *logos* — that horizon of intelligibility capsulized in the modern scientific revolution and the modern turn to the subject of Descartes and Kant and climaxing in the classic modern democratic revolutions and the emergence of modern historical consciousness — that no question could be allowed to be free of radical rethinking by so amazing a constellation of cultural strength and political-economic achievement united to equally amazing intellectual narrowness.

The reality of God was recast as a modern question in order to be properly understood by a modern mind. Those who still possessed a strong sense of God's reality as central to their lives became, as Michel de Certeau has shown, marginal to the modern centralizing project. Indeed such intensely religious persons became what moderns now called "mystics." An adjectival dimension to life and culture (the "mystical") now became a modern noun, the "mystic." This noun was used to name the large group of outsiders to the modern project. All reality must be disciplined by modern thought, including the reality of God and religion.

The modern God became the captive of one or another modern "ism." For the *logos* of modernity — its powerful notion of intelligibility — found a new way to understand God, more exactly a new series of ways. On the question of God, the modern mind had choices, to be sure. But all the modern choices were principally determined not by the reality of God but by the *logos* of modernity. A modern could, for example, be a deist or a modern theist or atheist or agnostic. A modern could become, with Spinoza, a modern pantheist, or, with Hegel and Whitehead, a modern panentheist.

There can be no doubt that these modern understandings of God yielded genuine insights into the reality of God. This is especially the case on the question of panentheism. For it was in modern theology — including modern Trinitarian theologies — that the intrinsically relational character of all reality, including, indeed especially, the divine reality, could be understood with the kind of conceptual clarity lacking in ancient and medieval "God-talk." Modern relational God-talk — Hegelian, process, Trinitarian, modern feminist — solidified as the one permanent achievement of modern theologies of God.

And yet even this now classic modern achievement came with a high price. In both Hegel and Whitehead, in many forms of modern relational thought (including several forms of feminist relational thought on God), the question recurs: is God rendered a conceptual prisoner of a new intellectual system of totality with no real moment of infinity allowing God to be God? Even that quintessential modern thinker, René Descartes, managed, almost despite himself, to allow God's infinity to break through his modern totality system. Does infinity break through Hegel or Whitehead or other contemporary modern forms of radically relational systematic (totalistic?) understandings of God?

Even modern theology's greatest achievement in understanding God — the relationality of God and all reality — was always in danger of becoming one more system, one of a long line of modern "isms." Those "isms" begin in early modernity, with an antirelational "deism" and end in late modernity with various relational forms of "panentheism." This is also the end of the contemporary story in the understanding of God unless one allows God's reality to break through the modern *logos* again. That breakthrough, indeed that radical interruption, is the central meaning of postmodern contemporary thought on God.

IV. Postmodernity and the Strange Return of God

By its attack upon the self-confidence of the modern *logos* post-modernity provided a new opportunity for serious contemporary thought on God. To be sure, much contemporary thought will continue to be modern in character and achievement; as in the sensitive and impressive reflections on God in cosmology and some of the "new physics" or in the renewed question of God for many modern scientists and theologians in their mutually informative conversations on science. Much contemporary thought on God, moreover, will prove to be a rediscovery of premodern forms for understanding God — as in the recent rediscovery of biblical narrative for Christian God-talk. At the same time, the most characteristically postmodern forms of God-talk have allowed the awe-some reality of *theos* to return in force after postmodernity's calling into question of modernity's powerful *logos*.

Indeed, postmodernity tends to be suspicious of almost all traditional and modern arguments on the existence and nature of God, all attempts to fit God's reality into a modern horizon of intelligibility, all of the famous modern "isms" for God from deism and theism through panentheism. Postmodern thought believes that too much of modernity's self-confidence as a *logos* is ill-conceived. Indeed the central meanings of two of the central categories in the modern *logos* — history and language — have been shattered by the analyses of postmodern thought.

First, history. Historical consciousness is one of the great discoveries and achievements of modern thought. Too often, however, that historical consciousness has included a not-so-secret narrative history of its own: a social evolutionary schema whereby all history leads to "the Western moderns." All else is prehistorical, or "primitive," or "archaic," or on its way to becoming another, if lesser, version of Western modernity.

History, on the modern schema, is a linear, continuous, teleological schema with a single *telos* — Western modernity. In such a schema, God (disguised as one or another modern "ism") is part of the schema: a sometimes important part (theism and panentheism) or sometimes missing part (atheism and agnosticism), but a part nonetheless. But what if history is not continuity at all but constituted by detours and labyrinths and radical interruptions? What if the modern social evolutionary teleological schema underlying modern self-understanding is exposed as both imperialist and implausible? Indeed modernity's sense of continuity and confidence has been shattered by two unassimilable elements — the interruption of massive global suffering in modern history and the interruption of all those others set aside, forgotten, and colonized by the grand narrative of Eurocentric modernity. The meaning of suffering, the reality of the others and the different: those are the realities that destroy the teleological version of modern history and allow for the return of the eschatological God disrupting all continuity and confidence.

God enters postmodern history not as a consoling "ism" but as an awesome, often terrifying, hope-beyond-hope. God enters history again not as a new speculation — even a modern Trinitarian one! — but as God. Let God be God becomes an authentic cry again. This God reveals God-self in hiddenness: in cross and negativity, above all in the suffering of all those others whom the grand narrative of modernity has set aside as non-peoples, non-events, non-memories, non-history.

God comes first as empowering hope to such peoples and theologies; a God promising to help liberate and transform all reality and promising as well to challenge and overcome the self-satisfied *logos* of modernity. God also comes to these postmodern forms of contemporary theology not only as the hidden-revealed God of the hope in the cross, in the memory of suffering and the struggle by, for, and with "others" — especially the forgotten and marginal ones of history. God also comes as an ever deeper Hiddenness — the awesome power, the terror, the hope beyond hopelessness often experienced in the struggle for liberation itself. Thus does the God of Job speak out of the whirlwind again in Gustavo Gutiérrez's profound later reflections on the hidden-revealed God. Thus does "suffering unto God" and lamentation toward God emerge as a resistance to all modern speculation on God in the post-Auschwitz, later political *theo-logia* of Johann Baptist Metz.[4] The hidden-revealed God at its most fearsome and radical has reentered theological thought again. But that entry is now not through the estranged and alienated self of the existentialist theologians, those admirable and deeply troubled moderns. The entry of the hidden-revealed God now comes through the interruptive experience and memory of suffering itself, the suffering of all those ignored, marginalized, and colonized by the grand narrative of modernity. In the light of that interruption, the modern "isms" for God suddenly seem somewhat inconsequential. Into that interruption the apocalyptic God of power, hope, and awe often becomes the God of Lamentation and Job returns to undo the power of the modern *logos* over "God" in contemporary theologies.

At the same time, the second category, language, has come in ever new and self-interrupting guises to disrupt modern thought in its own way. The very language which modern thought needs to think its horizon of intelligibility — its *logos*-centric *logos* rendering God into one more modern "ism" — disrupts modernity's sense of continuity and control. Through postmodern linguistic reflections on the unthought factors in modern thought, the modern *logos* dissolves its own former certainties and disowns its own self-presence and self-grounding. The modern self is not whole enough to be as purely autonomous as it once thought itself. The modern *logos* is not stable enough to control the reality of the God it once seemed to manage so easily through its arguments from modern reason. God returns to remove the "*theos*," at once grounding and domesticated, in modernity's onto-*theo*-logy. God returns to demand that modernity disown once and for all its speculative ambitions to control the divine reality in order to let God be God again.

Moreover, the two classic clues for understanding God's reality — love and intelligence — also return in new, postmodern forms and sometimes formlessness. "God is Love" now becomes an occasion not to show the reasonableness and relationality of the Divine Reality to the "modern mind." Love enters postmodernity first as transgression, then as excess, and finally as the transgressive excess of sheer gift.[5] To recover the great tradition of Dionysius the Areopagite again — the tradition of God beyond Being — is to call to task not merely that early and partial harbinger of modern rational theology, Thomas Aquinas, for his great reversal of the Dionysian order of "Good" over "Being" for naming God. To retrieve the Dionysian tradition is also to challenge modern theology in all its characteristic forms at the root. For the God who is Love is beyond being and transcendentality, beyond rationality and relationality. God is Love — excess, gift, the Good. That is a thought that modern theology cannot think without yielding its *logos* to *theos* in ways it does not seem to know how to do. Job and Lamentations return to haunt contemporary theologians as they attempt to name God in the new hidden-revealed theologies focused on history as interruption. So too such texts as the Song of Songs and the feminist retrievals of God as Sophia return to be heard in ways modern theologies did not envisage as even possible, much less desirable.[6] Desire, body, love, gift have all returned to allow God-as-God to be named anew.

When one turns to the second classical clue for understanding God, intelligence, the situation is the same: the modern *logos* in modern theology can no longer control God. Another kind of transgression and excess occurs: not new reflection on love as gift but the kind of radical detachment attendant to a profoundly apophatic theology like that of Meister Eckhart. These postmodern namings of a Godhead beyond God disclose modern theology's inability to envisage God beyond its own *logos*. Soon cries of atheism and Buddhism are heard.

But just as the tragic character of history emerges in the new apocalyptic theologies trying to recover Mark's gospel as well as Lamentations and Job, so too an insistence on attentiveness (that lost virtue and spiritual exercise) returns to clarify our contemporary needs. Indeed, in the apophatic piety of postmodern naming of God one can hear again what Simone Weil insisted moderns most needed to learn again: "attentiveness without an aim is the supreme form of prayer." Postmodern theology, at its best, is not a rival set of propositions to modern theology. It is something else: a search for entirely alternative forms. Even when speculative, postmodern thought is less propositional than it is an attempt at new forms of language rendering excess, gift, desire, prayer. The prayer and the forms can vary greatly from the attentiveness and detachment of apophaticism to the lamentation, awe, and sometimes terror of apocalypticism. This may not be so unhappy a message for modern theology to hear after all: to hear again Job and Lamentation, the Song of Songs and Sophia, to sense a Godhead beyond god and surely beyond the many "isms" created by and for the modern *logos*.

No one knows, I believe, where those postmodern suspicions and retrievals will finally lead. But this much is clear: amid all the shouting of the present, the reality of God has returned to the center of theology. This is not the time to rush out new propositions on the reality of God. This is rather the time to allow wonder again at the overwhelming mystery of God — as some physicists and cosmologists seem so much more skilled at doing than many theologians are. This is the time for theologians to learn to disallow the *logos* of modernity to control their thoughts on God as we learn anew to be attentive to God. We must learn somehow, in God's absent presence, to be still and know that God is God.

NOTES

1. Hans W. Frei, *The Identity of Jesus Christ* (Philadelphia: Fortress Press, 1975).

2. See the splendid work of Bernard Lonergan here: *Verbum: Word and Idea in Aquinas* (London: Darton Longman and Todd, 1968).

3. Louis Dupré, *Passage to Modernity: An Essay in the Hermeneutics of Nature and Culture* (New Haven: Yale University Press, 1994).

4. Johann Baptist Metz, "Suffering unto God" forthcoming in *Critical Inquiry* (Summer 1995). See also Gustavo Gutiérrez, *On Job: God-Talk and the Suffering of the Innocent* (Maryknoll: Orbis Books, 1987).

5. See Jean-Luc Marion, *God without Being* (Chicago: University of Chicago Press, 1993).

6. Elizabeth Johnson, *She Who Is: The Mystery of God in Feminist Theological Discourse* (New York: Crossroad, 1992).

4

God of History, God of Psychology

I. Resurrection and Reincarnation

If resurrection is actual, history is real. If God raised Jesus of Nazareth from the dead, all is changed. Resurrection faith does not remove one from history but for it. The hope of human beings is not merely life after death but a hope for history itself. For the God who raised Jesus from the dead is the God who acted in the history of ancient Israel and in the history of Jesus. That same God will act in history and beyond it to save the living and the dead. The fact that God — the origin, sustainer, and end of all reality — acts in history becomes the heart of Christian faith and thereby hope in history.

The great religious traditions of Hinduism and Buddhism find neither resurrection nor history at the heart of their different envisionments of Ultimate Reality and the role of *karma* in human existence. As Christians finally begin to learn from these great classical ways, we surely need a humility in understanding and learning from their central beliefs (including *karma* and reincarnation), which we have too often lacked. For example, where in all our Western speculative traditions can one find a debate as sophisticated as the many Hindu debates on the use of impersonal or personal language for naming Ultimate Reality? Even the debates focused upon Spinoza and Fichte can begin to seem relatively simple compared to the classic debates in Hinduism centered upon Shankara and Ramanuja. Even Derrida can seem *simpliste* compared to the subtleties on the inadequacy of all language and all dialectic in the great Buddhist thinker Nagarjuna.

Source: *Concilium* 1993/5, *Reincarnation or Resurrection*, edited by Hermann Häring and Johann Baptist Metz.

47

Or where may we find the sheer variety, even excess, in images for the divine that one finds with such abundance and power in the classic myths and symbols of Hinduism? Where can we find in all our Western traditions a more emancipatory discovery of the transience of all reality than one finds in Buddhism? Through Buddhist meditative practices, Christians too can learn to let go of their compulsive clinging. And where can modern Westerners find in their own traditions the subtle classic Hindu and Buddhist understandings of the interweaving of all human responsibilities with the cosmos itself through *karma*, rebirth, and emancipation from the cycle of death and rebirth? Surely not in modern Western vulgarizations of these beliefs in "new age" understandings of reincarnation.

It is a strange irony that we seem to face now in any serious Christian theological attempt at understanding anew either resurrection or reincarnation and their real differences and similarities. At exactly the moment when some Christian theologians finally begin to listen to and study Hinduism and Buddhism with the care they so clearly need, one finds many contemporary Hindus and especially Buddhists rethinking the nature of *karma* and thereby reincarnation as well as rethinking their relationship to history. The interreligious dialogue on these issues can seem suddenly very promising indeed (see Masao Abe, Hans Küng, and John Cobb). And yet at the very moment when a genuine interreligious dialogue could begin anew (including a serious dialogue on resurrection and reincarnation analogous to the previous ancient Greek Christian dialogue on immortality and resurrection) we may find ourselves strangely impeded. For the Christian hope in resurrection has too often been dissipated in modern Christianity into yet another reward for the compulsive ego empowering so much contemporary religiousness. At the same time the classic Hindu and Buddhist and even Platonic beliefs in reincarnation are surely in danger of being misunderstood at best and vulgarized at worst by being torn from their classic contexts and rethought as new hope for the same modern Western ego.

Both resurrection and reincarnation are in danger of becoming contemporary beliefs torn from their classical contexts of meaning and truth in order to become living options for all-consuming modern egos. The secret of these revisionary readings of both resurrection and reincarnation is not so hard to see: the ego is what finally counts; whatever belief helps to encourage and secure that ego will be embraced as true religion; anything that disorients and threatens the ego will be rejected (like the God who raised Jesus from the dead and acts

in history for the oppressed; like classical Hindu and Buddhist profound distrust of the ego and thereby profound misgivings on the
cycle of birth, death and rebirth, reincarnation).

If a belief in God enters an ego-centered religion at all, it will be as
the secret aim or projection of the ego's desires and drives. Contemporary religiousness is the ultimate triumph of Feuerbach. Religion
will be approved. But resurrection of this failed Jesus of Nazareth?
History as disruption? God as the dangerous God of history? All such
counteregoistic realities will quietly pass out of notice as the truly
dangerous God of history passes into a no longer dangerous memory
as a vague hope of our ever more distant ancestors. The question that
recurs for serious Christian theologians today — the question disrupting any easy contemporary talk of resurrection or reincarnation
— is, as it always was, the question of God — the God of history and
the God of authentic psychology as well.

II. The Hidden-Revealed God of History

It is a theological commonplace that the biblical God is the God
who acts in history. For the Christian the decisive manifestation of
the identity of this God is revealed in the person and event of Jesus
the Christ. Through Jesus Christ, Christians understand anew the
reality of God as the God of history: the God who acted in the Exodus
history of ancient Israel is the same God who acted and thereby
decisively manifested God-self in the ministry and message, the passion, the death and resurrection of this unsubstitutable Jesus of Nazareth.

But how may contemporary Christians best understand this God
who acts in the history of Jesus Christ? In one sense, modern progressive Christian theology has been an attempt to answer that question.
Sometimes the answer has been divorced from the actual history of
the Jesus in and through whom God has decisively disclosed the God
who acts in history. The emergence of historical consciousness and
thereby the development and use of historical-critical methods in the
Bible has proved to be, like all human achievements, ambiguous in
its effects upon modern Christian understandings of God and history.
On the one hand, the results of the historical-critical method have
freed Christians to be both more careful and more cautious in their
claims for the historical character of the events (whether Exodus, Si-

nai, or the history of Jesus) related by the Bible. On the other hand, the use of historical-critical methods sometimes removes Christians from paying sufficient attention to the details of the history of Israel and the history of Jesus as those details were narrated by the first communities — above all, for the Christian, in the passion narratives of the New Testament.[1]

This characteristically modern loss of attention to the disclosure of the God of history in the narrative details of the passion and the resurrection narratives can be a loss, as many new narrative theologies argue, of the heart of the matter on where to look first for understanding the God of history. As the famous poetic rule observes: God is to be found in the details. Which details? For the Christian, above all, the details narrated by the first Christian communities on this Jesus they proclaimed as the Christ: the narrative details of the ministry and message, the passion, death, and resurrection of Jesus of Nazareth. Who is God? God is the one who raised this disgraced Jesus from the dead and vindicated his ministry and message, his life and his person as the Christ and, as Jesus Christ, the very manifestation of who God is and who we are commanded and empowered to become. Christians may now understand themselves as commanded and empowered to find God above all in and through the historical struggle for justice and love — the historical struggle for the living and the dead — proleptically vindicated through the resurrection of Jesus.

Surely the great liberation movements and theologies of our period are the theologies that best teach us all the dangerous truth of the God of history. For the liberation theologians, starting with Gustavo Gutiérrez's brilliant reading of the Exodus narrative, know that the God of history is to be found, above all, in those great narratives of total liberation and hope.

In the liberation, political, and feminist theologians, Christian theology articulates anew its faith in the God of concrete history.[2] This liberating God of history is not identical to the God of modern historical consciousness — a consciousness often driven by an unconscious desire to replace the biblical narratives on the God who acts in history with a modern social-evolutionary narrative that may comfort modern religiousness but seems incapable of manifesting any dangerous God of concrete history.

The God of concrete history is also not identical to the God of existentialist and transcendental historicity. The latter God of historicity is disclosed by an analysis of the existential and transcendental conditions of possibility of the modern historical subject. However, this God of historicity seems far removed from the dangerous and disruptive God of the history narrated in Exodus and in the history of Jesus.

What a curious fate modern Christian theologies of history have undergone! Guided by the honest belief that they were taking history with full seriousness, many theologians began to develop either theologies of historical consciousness (Troeltsch) or theologies of historicity (Bultmann). These were and are serious and honorable enterprises. And yet the questions recur. Where is the God of history in these modern theologies of historicity and historical consciousness? Where is the history of Israel and above all the history of Jesus embedded in the biblical narratives? Where are the actual conflicts, sufferings, and memories of oppression that constitute history as the struggle for justice, freedom, and love? Where is resurrection as the hope for the vindication in history and beyond history of all the living and the dead? Where are the victims of history to whom the God of history narrated in the history of Jesus speaks as distinct from the victors who write the histories informing modern historical consciousness?

It would be foolish to turn against the genuine, indeed permanent, achievements of the great modern theologies of historical consciousness and historicity. In these theologies we can find the fruits of the great modern experiment: a defense of freedom and rights, an insistence on truthfulness, an honest rejection of the triumphalism of many traditional theologies of history from Eusebius through Bossuet and beyond in favor of the honest, critical, cautious correctives of traditional accounts by the use of historical-critical methods. Surely these accomplishments are one of the permanent achievements of modernity. However, we are now at a point in history where the underside of modernity, the dialectic of Enlightenment, must also be honestly acknowledged.

For there is an underside to all the talk about history in modern religion and theology. That underside is revealed in the shocking silence in theologies of historical consciousness and historicity alike on the victims of history. The history of modern progressive theologies of history is too often a history without radical interruption, without a memory of the victims of history, without a consciousness of patriarchy, or racism or classism or Eurocentrism, without Auschwitz, Hiroshima, or the Gulag. Modern progressive theologies of history are always in danger of becoming religionized narratives of some other story than the disruptive and disturbing narrative of the fate and resurrection of Jesus the Christ.

At their best modern theologies of history articulate the great continuities of history. In this relatively optimistic account of the teleological continuities of history, modern theologies of history bear
certain analogies to Luke-Acts. And yet even Luke's Gospel, with all
its belief in history's fundamental continuity, adds the undertow of
the inevitability of Jesus' fate best rendered in Luke by his brilliant
use of the journey motif to show how Jesus must end in Jerusalem.

Many theologies of history, however Lukan in their emphasis on
continuity and teleology, read history in a manner different from the
more cautious Lukan narrative: history is freed of conflict and interruption and even the inevitability of suffering to become an evolutionary schema that somehow leads teleologically to Western
modernity; the resurrection seems to become a purely personal, not
historical, matter even as eschatology is removed from history and
placed with the "last things" of the individual; the resurrection is, in a
second fatal step, divorced from the cross and its disruptive history
and allowed to drift quietly into either silence or as identical to some
notion of either immortality or even reincarnation.

There are, however, other theologians who have rediscovered the
genuine God of history as the hidden-revealed God. For God's principal revelation is in hiddenness. This hiddenness includes, to be sure,
the suffering, conflict and estrangement within the self — the dilemma of hiddenness so brilliantly articulated from Paul through Augustine, Luther, Pascal, Kierkegaard, and the great existentialist theologians of our century.

However, as the political, feminist, and liberation theologians im-
ply, the principal revelation of God is not in the hiddenness of the
cross, conflict, struggle, negativity as manifested in the private alienated self.

If contemporary theology is to understand the God of history and
not the God projected by its own desires for continuity and triumph,
we must turn anew to the hidden-revealed God of history. The secretly evolutionary schemas in modern historical consciousness, the
careless discarding of the revelatory details of the biblical narratives
of the history of Jesus in favor of some new historically-reconstructed
narrative of the historical Jesus, the strangely ahistorical concept of
historicity of the modern subject of theology: all these theologies of
the God of history must yield to the hidden-revealed God of the great
biblical narratives of the God of history.

Even earlier biblical theologies of "the God who acts in history"
(von Rad, Wright) are no longer adequate to disclose the disturbing

and interruptive hiddenness of the God who does act in history. For the all too continuous schemas of "salvation-history" abstracted, above all, from the so-called Yahwist narratives of the Old Testament and the Luke-Acts narratives of the New Testament may prove too easily coopted by the three great corrupters of this emancipatory biblical schema: fundamentalist literalism, social-evolutionary modernism, or ecclesiastical triumphalism.

In biblical categories, the hidden-revealed God of history is best seen not in Luke but in the God of Mark's apocalyptic Gospel. The God of history is present through absence — as in the seeming absence of his Father to Mark's Jesus on the cross, the Jesus who cries from the cross the cry of all the victims of real history: "My God, my God, why have you forsaken me?" This God of history is often present through absence. And yet something else also occurs in Mark's affirmation of resurrection — the seemingly absent God of Jesus' cry from the cross becomes the hidden-revealed God of the brief Markan resurrection account.

But the very reticence of Mark on resurrection united to his insistence on the centrality of cross, suffering, and conflict occurs in the hiddenness of his apocalyptic vision of history as interruption, not continuity. Mark's God of history is disclosed in genuine hiddenness: the hiddenness of the conflict, struggle, negativity, suffering, cross which is actual history to the victims of history. This is the history which Mark shows to all those clear-headed enough to view history not with the eyes of the victors who write history[3] but with the new apocalyptic vision provided by the God who vindicated this Jesus whom the God of history raised from the dead. It is hardly surprising that the great liberation theologies of our day can move (as does Gustavo Gutiérrez) from the liberating historical hope for justice of the Exodus narrative to the occasional collapse of all one's hopes in Job.[4] Such a remarkable range for understanding the hidden-revealed God of history in both Exodus and Job is possible for all theologians ready to understand the God of history as the hidden-revealed God decisively manifested in the passion narratives (especially Mark) as those narratives are read in the context of the struggle of all those — living and dead — who have experienced the God of history revealed in the hiddenness of the history of Jesus — in the narrated gospel details of his ministry and message, his fate, his conflict with authorities, his table-fellowship with sinners, his suffering, cross, and resurrection.

III. The Incomprehensible-Comprehensible God of Psychology

In the context of the revelation of the God of history in the history of
Jesus of Nazareth, Christians also discover new psychological and
theological understanding of the self: as a historical subject responsi-
ble to self and others before the God of history; responsible to the
struggle for justice and freedom in history because capable of responding to the God of history. As the New Testament itself suggests,
there are further insights into the reality of the self which Christian
reflection upon the God of history and the self as a historical subject
suggests. Surely Augustine and Luther, Pascal and Kierkegaard were
not wrong to insist upon the introspective self as an always troubled,
often estranged self living in and through the dialectic of grace and
sin. That understanding of the self, unknown in its intensity of intro-
spection to the ancients, comes to light (as Paul's great paradoxes
and dialectical language show) through the dialectic of the hidden-
revealed God disclosed in the history of the Crucified One. What a
modern observer might name the psychological dilemmas of the self
are sharpened by the harsh light cast upon the inevitability of sin
and, above all, the reality of grace made available by the God revealed
in the crucified one. The God of history, properly construed, is also
the God of the authentic self and thereby the God of psychology.

Nor are Christians left only with the extraordinary models for understanding the dilemmas of the self forged by Paul's great reflections
on the self in the light of the hidden God revealed in the crucified
one. As the Christian search for wisdom and love also becomes a
search for the authentic self, Christians begin to articulate their vision
of the essential self alive even in the midst of radical estrangement. At
the same time, other images and understandings of God may occur
to Christian reflection.

It is hardly surprising in our psychological cultures that even political, liberation, and feminist theologians, without abandoning for a
moment their focus on the God of history, can also engage, under the
rubric of a mystical-political faith, in a further search for the true self
in the light of the God of wisdom and love. Thereby does theology
also turn to psychology. Here feminist theologies, with the insight
that the personal is also the political, have taught all theology the
deepest lessons.

As many studies have shown, modern psychology has much to

teach and to learn from the great traditions of spirituality on God and the self. The classical biblical wisdom traditions as well as the later mystical traditions have returned in our period with power to deepen Christian understanding of the reality of God and thereby also the reality of the self.

This development begins, in fact, in the New Testament itself. For the movement to a wisdom reading of the history of Jesus is the great accomplishment of the Johannine tradition. Indeed it is little wonder that the classical Christian mystical traditions — the image mystics, Trinitarian mystics, love mystics, and apophatic mystics — all appeal to the Gospel of John to clarify the reality of the God disclosed in the reality of the *logos*.

The Johannine tradition first articulates the central Christian metaphor "God is Love" (I John 4.8). Reflection on that metaphor will allow the wisdom and mystical traditions further insights into the interrelated realities of God, the cosmos, history, and the true self. If there is a true "God of psychology" for Christians, that God may be found only by meditation on the God of history hidden and revealed in the history of Jesus. That God is the God of wisdom and love informing and transforming all human psychological understanding of wisdom and love taught by all those spiritual exercises faithful to the God of the Word, the Form, the *logos*, the Image of the God who is Love and Wisdom.

It is true that our modern psychological culture concentrates far too much attention upon human subjectivity and personal experience. In that sense modern psychology can obscure not only the God of history but also the God of wisdom and love. The God of the wisdom trajectories of both Testaments and the God of the mystics does provide profound new insights into the true self. However, the wisdom traditions and the mystical traditions (and, *a fortiori*, the prophetic traditions) always place the search for personal experience and the authentic self within the context of an understanding of the God of wisdom and love and thereby the relationship not merely of the self to itself (as in modern individualism) but of the self to others, history, the cosmos, and, above all, to God. As Michel de Certeau argued,[5] there are clear historical reasons why the mystics of early modernity needed to use such person-centered subjective language in order to articulate their wisdom on the self's experience of God. There are devastating losses whenever any psychology of individualism robs the Christian wisdom and mystical traditions of their central insight: the authentic self, for the Christian, is never an individual in the modern individualist sense but always a person with individual dignity, to be sure, but a person constituted by her/his relationships to others, to history and the struggle for justice, to the cosmos, and above all to the God of history and the God of wisdom and love. And in fidelity to that prior understanding of God Christians can speak of the God of psychology and the authentic psychological self.

From this perspective the modern development of psychology can also be construed as a positive development for the theological understanding of God and self. As Sebastian Moore has argued,[6] modern psychology can aid theology greatly by its clarification of the psychological realities of the self seeking wisdom and love grounded in meditations proper to the history of Jesus. In that sense, there is every good reason to be encouraged by the mystical and thereby also the psychological elements in the new mystical-political theologies.

Insofar as Christians speak of the God of wisdom and love, they may also speak of a God of psychology. But this Christian construal of a God of psychology cannot be one more projection of the modern ego. That God could be related neither to the God of history nor to the God of wisdom and love. However, the God of wisdom and love is, for Christians, also the God who teaches new truths about the true self. Christian theologians of the patristic and medieval periods, for example, reflected upon intelligence as a principal clue in humans to some understanding of God as pure intelligence and wisdom.

Moreover, as Christians also reflected on the classic metaphor "God is love" (itself grounded in the history of Jesus as disclosive of the God who is love), they found themselves more and more clearly Trinitarian Christians who understood the God manifested in the history of Jesus as the only God there is — the triune God who is love. Several modern forms of theology (like Hegel and process theology) can be viewed as profound modern reflections on the intrinsically relational character of the divine reality who is love. Some postmodern forms of theology (like the powerful new theology of Jean-Luc Marion)[7] can be viewed as characteristically postmodern reflections on love not as relationality but as excess — and also as postmodern retrievals of the classic Christian neo-Platonist metaphors of God's love as overflow.

As the love of God which is excess and the wisdom of God which is ultimately incomprehensible through its very excess, a new Christian vision of God as the comprehensible-incomprehensible One has emerged once again in all Christian meditation on God. As Karl Rahner made clear in his final essays on God, God's incomprehensibility is a fully positive characteristic of God's own reality, not merely a commentary on human finitude and ignorance. Such an understanding of the incomprehensible God, moreover, frees the Christian to become, as Rahner insisted, the most radical skeptic in modernity — skeptical, above all, about modernity's pretensions to certainty, especially any presumed certainty about finally understanding the self.

The God of history, thanks to the remarkable achievements of the political, liberation, and feminist theologians, can now be viewed as the God revealed in the history of Jesus, i.e., the history of the God revealed in the hiddenness of suffering, negativity, cross. By empowering human beings to become agents of history rather than either passive recipients of whatever happens or modern compulsive egos, the new vision of God also frees the "mystical" part of the mystical-political option to its own new understanding of God as love — a love so excessive it is ultimately incomprehensible.

There is no need, therefore, to choose between history and psychology. Rather one should follow a path of disciplined spiritual exercises aiding one's understanding of the God of wisdom and love (and, in that sense, also of psychology). This spiritual path follows, not precedes, the path of discipleship to the God of history revealed in the history of Jesus. A fidelity to the fullness of that history is a fidelity to history itself as the decisive locus of God's self-revelation. In that context of the hidden-revealed God of history, all later reflections on the authentic self occur. Such reflections may be occasioned by the wisdom of the ancient Greeks or, more recently, the classic wisdom of the great Hindu and Buddhist traditions or the clear grains of modern psychologies. All wisdom from all sources should be welcomed by Christian theology as long as that wisdom is open to transformation by an understanding of the incomprehensible God of wisdom and love as that understanding of God is in turn grounded in a prior prophetic understanding of the hidden-revealed God of History.

NOTES

1. See Hans Frei, *The Eclipse of Biblical Narrative* (New Haven 1974).

2. Representative works include Elizabeth Johnson, *She Who Is: The Mystery of God in Feminist Theological Discourse* (New York 1992); Peter Hodgson, *God in History: Shapes of Freedom* (Nashville 1989); Gustavo Gutiérrez, *The God of Life* (London and Maryknoll 1991); Johann Baptist Metz, *Faith in*

History and Society: Toward a Practical Fundamental Theology (New York 1980).

3. This insight into history has been articulated with power in the well-known reflections on history and its victims by Walter Benjamin, Simone Weil, and Johann Baptist Metz. It is their reflections which have most informed my own on this question.

4. Compare Gustavo Gutiérrez, *A Theology of Liberation: History, Politics, and Salvation* (Maryknoll 1973; London 1974), and *On Job: God-Talk and the Suffering of the Innocent* (Maryknoll 1987).

5. Michel de Certeau, *La Fable Mystique* (Paris 1982).

6. Sebastian Moore, *The Crucified Jesus Is No Stranger* (New York and London 1977); *The Fire and the Rose Are One* (New York and London 1980).

7. Jean-Luc Marion, *God without Being* (Chicago 1991).

Part Three

Contemporary Theological Issues

5

The Holocaust as Interruption
and the Christian Return to History

In the early modern period, the major historical events for new forms of Christian theology (liberal and modernist) were those two linked intellectual and historical explosions: the eighteenth-century Enlightenment and the nineteenth-century rise of historical consciousness. These events were clearly historical events in the usual sense of the emergence of new groupings of power, new institutions, and new concrete struggles. Nevertheless both events lent themselves more readily than the historical events of the twentieth century to a seemingly more intellectual, even "academic," set of theological questions. Perhaps the deceptively ahistorical character that many intellectuals accorded these events tempted Christian theology in that liberal period to focus its intentions less on concrete history and more on the seemingly ahistorical crisis of cognitive claims in Christian self-understanding (and especially the crisis of historical claims occasioned by critiques of the Enlightenment and the rise of historical consciousness). The theological major shift of interest in the last two centuries to the symbol of "revelation" as the major symbol for theological attention is merely the clearest illustration of the kind of sea-change which occurred.

Indeed, as such atypical theologians in that period as Soren

This article originally appeared in *Concilium* 1984/5 as an editorial signed by Elisabeth Schüssler-Fiorenza and David Tracy. The present reprint includes only the first part of the article, i.e., the part written by David Tracy. Elisabeth Schüssler-Fiorenza's reflections (the second part) may be found in the issue. The authors consulted with each other during the writing of this editorial.

Kierkegaard saw, Christianity was in danger of becoming so exclusively a religion of cognitive "revelation" that its function as primarily a religion of concrete "salvation" could seem in doubt. This problem of a liberal retreat from concrete history was compounded by the fact that liberal optimism on cognitive meaning (and hence revelation) yielded theologies of salvation which functioned largely as theologies of triumphant intellectual reconciliation. The tragic irony soon became apparent: the very discovery of historical consciousness and the attendant theological furor with the crisis of the "cognitive" claims tempted theology to retreat from history itself. It was Hegel's dialectical optimism, not his observation that history was a slaughter-bench, that largely won the liberal day. The gains of the historico-critical method and the classic liberal and modernist theologies which they occasioned are plain for all to see. But the loss — the loss of concrete history itself under the paradoxical cover of "historical consciousness" — was a loss whose full impact we are just beginning to realize.

It is true that neo-orthodox theology — here understood as a self-critical moment within the liberal tradition — did correct the liberals at several crucial points. Above all, Karl Barth's rediscovery of the "strange, new world of the Bible" can now be seen for what it was: a hermeneutic rediscovery of the fact that the subject matter — the strange new world of the Christ-event to which all theology, including the scriptures, witnesses — must control all theological interpretation. This theological rediscovery was itself partly occasioned, as is well known, by the shattering impact of the First World War on earlier liberal optimism and self-confidence.

And what the neo-orthodox learned must still be honored: the recognition of radical *historicity* beyond all liberal and optimistic senses of historical consciousness; the acknowledgment that, theologically, the subject matter of the eschatological event must rule; the insistence that this subject matter forces a rediscovery of the need for *Sachkritik* in the scriptures themselves. The most enduring aspect of Bultmann's demythologizing program, for example, was not his concern with the cognitive dilemmas that modernity posed for Christian self-understanding (that theology already learned from the earlier liberals and modernists). Bultmann's greatest contribution was his insistence that the eschatological event to which the scriptures witness enforces — within the scriptures and upon all later interpreters — a radical demythologizing. What was said in the scriptures must be judged critically by what was truly meant.

And yet even these characteristically neo-orthodox moves rarely brought Christian theology into concrete history. Rather the vertical transcendence of the neo-orthodox understanding of the eschatological event encouraged a theology increasingly privatized and thereby increasingly remote from the slaughter-bench of history itself. For no less than the liberals, the neo-orthodox theologians often entered history atheologically. Where the very discovery of historical consciousness paradoxically impeded the liberals' entry into history, radical historicity and the hermeneutic rediscovery of the absolutely transcendent character of the eschatological event just as paradoxically impeded a neo-orthodox entry into history — including, indeed especially, on the question of the Jewish people in Nazi Germany.

Karl Barth stated clearly in 1966, "We do not wish to forget that there is ultimately only one really central ecumenical question: that is our relationship to Judaism." As profound as that statement is on Christian theological grounds, it must still be asked: But what can this mean when that overwhelming historical event of the modern West — the Holocaust — is not accorded any theological weight?

What can it mean when this interruption in and to our history occurs? What can it mean for humanist liberal theologians and neo-orthodox Christian theologians alike when the history they theologically ignore crashes against itself in the horror of the Holocaust? Is there to be no *Sachkritik* here — and here alone? Is the question of Judaism — stated as the ecumenical question — a question to be divorced from the fate of the reality empowering all Jewish thought — the Jewish people?

Christian theologians of the modern period have honestly come to terms with the new senses of historical consciousness and historicity in the unsettling events of the eighteenth and nineteenth centuries. They have developed a theological hermeneutics where the subject matter — the event itself — is once again allowed to rule in theological hermeneutic. They have recognized the *Sachkritik* that the eschatological event itself demands. But they have too seldom returned to history — the real, concrete thing where events like the Holocaust have happened.

There is, in contemporary Christian theology, one great exception to these observations: the political, the feminist, and the liberation theologies. For behind the deprivatizing demands of these theologies and behind their insistence on the priority of praxis over theory, behind their retrieval of the great suspicions lurking in half-forgotten, even repressed eschatological symbols, lies their single-minded and constant refrain: Christian theology must move past both liberal historical consciousness and neo-orthodox hermeneutical historicity and move again — as theology — into the concrete history of suffering and oppression. These theologies do not mean by history theories of historiography nor philosophies of history. They do not mean a purely vertical transcendence where history becomes a tangent, a theological accident. They mean history: they mean the concrete struggles of groups, societies, persons, victims, who have been shunted aside from the official story of triumph. They mean that the central theological question today is not the question of the nonbeliever but the question of the nonperson — those forgotten ones, living and dead, whose struggle and memory are our history.

It is the singular achievement of these feminist, liberation, and political theologians that their theological return into history — more exactly into the history of those whom official historical accounts including Christian theological accounts have disowned as nonpersons, nongroups, nonhistory — has empowered these new theologies. As theologies they retrieve, in and through their very suspicions, the repressed moments of the New Testament such as the profound negations in the genre of apocalyptic — so embarrassing to the liberals, so unnecessary to neo-orthodox eschatologies.

Central in these theologies is the retrieval of the sense of history as interruption, as rupture, break, discontinuity in apocalyptic, the retrieval of liberation over easy announcements of reconciliation, the retrieval of the social systemic expression of sin over individual sins, the retrieval of the concrete praxis of discipleship. Given all this, there is yet more urgency for all theology to face the interruption of the Holocaust. For is it possible for any of us to insist upon the need for a Christian theological return to concrete history yet not face that? And if Christian theologians do face that historical caesura, can any of us any longer easily retrieve the "fulfillment" theme always in danger of becoming a supercessionist theme, the lack of theological anger at Matthew 25 or the use of "the Jews" in John's gospel, the uninterrupted use of traditional law-gospel motifs?

If Christian theology is to enter history, then surely this interruption of the Holocaust is a frightening disclosure of the real history within which we have lived. The theological fact is that Christian theology cannot fully return to history until it faces the Holocaust. It cannot face that interruption in history without facing as well the anti-Semitic effects of its own Christian history. It cannot face that interruption without realizing that the return to history must now be the return through the radical negativity disclosed by that event. All the retrievals of those authoritative and formerly repressed themes which empower a theological return must yield to the radical *Sachkritik* which the eschatological event itself demands. Every hermeneutics of retrieval for Christian theology must today include a radical hermeneutics of suspicion on the whole of Christian history.

6

Exodus

Theological Reflection

There is no paradigm more central to Judaism than Exodus and Sinai. The history of the reception of this great paradigm by the rabbinic commentators to Jewish theologians and other scholars, writers, and activists today is at the heart of the Jewish tradition. It is possible to read Genesis as the story of individuals and families in relationship to God. But the story of Exodus — the classic narrative of bondage in Egypt, the promised land, the murmurings in the wilderness, the covenant at Sinai, the leadership of Moses and Aaron, the struggle for a better life in the promised land — is the story of a people. It is the heart of the Hebrew Scriptures. Exodus is the story which the great prophets retell and develop in and for later times. It is that story which the development of Messianism and later apocalyptic and wisdom traditions try either to radicalize or deflect from its centrality to the whole Bible. The great narrative of Exodus as told in the books of Exodus, Deuteronomy, and Numbers is the narrative of a people who have been called to struggle in the wilderness and have been promised a new covenant and a new land but not paradise: a realistic, this-worldly promise, this promise of a better land in Canaan to become a liberated people, Israel. The history of Jewish thought and Jewish existence as the people of the Covenant is the history of the memory and life of the event and texts of Exodus.

There is also no paradigm that should be more central to Christian

Source: *Concilium* 1987/1 (no. 189), *Exodus: A Lasting Paradigm*, edited by Bas van Iersel and Anton Weiler

self-understanding than Exodus. At least when Christians remain faithful to their Jewish roots, Exodus becomes central to their consciousness. For it is Exodus which provides a proper context for understanding the great Christian paradigm of the life-ministry-death-and-resurrection of Jesus Christ. In a sense, this Christian paradigm — with its many contexts from Old Testament traditions of Messianism, wisdom, and apocalyptic — is most faithful to itself when it does not allow the dehistoricizing and depoliticizing of Jesus Christ. Christianity is most itself when it is an Exodus religion.

The rise of political theology, liberation theology, and feminist theology in our period shows the reemergence of the paradigm of Exodus as a central context (with its covenant of Sinai and its reinterpretations by the great prophets) for understanding the central text and event of Christian reality — the ministry, life and message, death and resurrection of Jesus the Christ. When Christian self-understanding is tempted to depoliticize its self-understanding and praxis, Christians need only reflect on Exodus as the paradigm which should inform and transform the highly personal but not individualist Christian self-understanding in the light of the reality of the death and resurrection of Jesus Christ. When Christian theology is tempted to flee to other-worldly theology, it is able to turn to neo-Platonism and even to some strands of the wisdom traditions of both Testaments. But it cannot turn to Exodus. For Exodus demands a resolutely this-worldly spirituality as it demands a historical and political, not a private or individualist, understanding of Christian salvation-as-total-liberation. Finally, when Christian theology is tempted to despair of biblical realism for its political theology one can turn to the narrative of Exodus. For Exodus disallows both millennarianism and despair.

I. No Text without History

Exodus, like any classic religious paradigm, has given rise to profound plurality and ambiguity in its reception, in both theory and practice, in religious and secular thought alike. Jew or Christian, in their differing ways, will profoundly affirm their covenantal trust in God's actions in Exodus and their hope for divine empowerment and their realization of the demand for the human historical struggle for total liberation. A Jew or a Christian will also face the ambiguities of the reception of the paradigm of Exodus in their histories. The Hebrew Scriptures can be read as a series of sometimes complementary, sometimes conflicting interpretations of Exodus, Sinai, and Covenant. Who any longer claims to find a fully coherent "biblical theology" in these scriptures?

As modern hermeneutics with its notion of *Wirkungsgeschichte* makes clear, no text comes to us as purely autonomous. It comes bearing with it the history of its former receptions in theory and practice. In the case of Exodus, those receptions include all those — Jewish, Christian, secular — which have gone before us and all those in our own day. There is no honest theological way to avoid that reality nor to shirk the need to face the plurality and ambiguity of the reality of the reception of the paradigm and classic texts of Exodus in our history: from empowerment of the ancient Israelites as a people to the terrible fate of the Canaanites and the "murmurers" among the Israelites themselves; from the struggle for political freedom by Cromwell and his followers to the fate of the Irish Catholics trapped in his self-righteous and revolting path; from the "noble experiment" of the New England Puritans and the fate of the natives of North America (those still misnamed "Indians"). In our own time one cannot forget either the present noble struggle of the use of Exodus in the liberation theologies of Latin America nor the frightening use of that same paradigm for taking the "land" and for treating Black Africans as the "Canaanites" among some South African Reformed theologians. Even Exodus is not an innocent text. This reality forces all theologians to realize that theology itself must now pay greater attention in all its interpretations to the pluralistic and ambiguous reception of all its classic texts, including Exodus.

History is not only contingent: history is interruptive. Western history is, through and through, an interruptive narrative with no single theme and no controlling plot. To be an American, for example, can be to live with pride by participating in a noble experiment of freedom and plurality. But to be a white American is also to belong to a history, partly through one use of the Exodus symbol, that includes the near-destruction of one people (the North American "Indians," the true Native Americans) and the enslavement of another people (the African Americans). Not to honor the ancient Greeks as our ancestors is possible only for those who lack any sense of true greatness. But to honor and belong to the Greeks is also to acknowledge the interruptions in their, i.e. our, history: the role of the other as barbarian; the vindictive policies of imperialist Athens toward Melos and other colonies; the unexamined role of women and slaves in the polis; the cries of the Athenians themselves in the quarries of Syracuse.

Similarly, to claim the ancient Israelites as our predecessors or Exodus as our theme is an honor. But that claim also forces us to face the patriarchal nature of that society. We cannot forget what the Israelites of the Exodus did to the Canaanites and the murmurers among the Israelites and what their prayers against the children of their enemies might mean. To cherish the New Testament as a charter document of Exodus-liberation in cross and resurrection is entirely right. Yet we must also face its anti-Judaic strands in some of its "new Covenant" and "new Exodus" language: strands that reach us with the full history of the effects of centuries of Christian "teaching of contempt" for the Jews. And we have just begun to face the centuries of subjugation of women in Jewish and Christian history — indeed, in most accounts of the Exodus itself (see Deuteronomy 29:10-13).

II. Ambiguity

No classic text like Exodus comes to us without the plural and ambiguous history of effects of its own production and all its former receptions. Nor does any classic event, be it the Renaissance, the Reformation, or the Enlightenment — or the event Exodus. "Every great work of civilization," as Walter Benjamin insisted, "is at the same time a work of barbarism." Plurality seems an adequate word to suggest the extraordinary variety which any study of language shows and any study of the variety of receptions of any classic documents. Ambiguity may be too mild a word to describe the strange mixture of great good and frightening evil that our history reveals. And yet, at least until more adequate and probably new words are coined, ambiguity will have to suffice.

Historical ambiguity means that a once seemingly clear historical narrative of progressive Western enlightenment and emancipation has now become a montage of classics and newspeak, of startling beauty and revolting cruelty, of partial emancipation and ever more subtle forms of entrapment. Ambiguous is certainly one way to describe our history and our interpretations of such classics as Exodus. At one time we may have believed realistic and even naturalistic narratives of the triumphs of the West. But these traditional narratives are now overlaid not only with modernist narratives and their occasional epiphanies amid the mass of historical confusion, but also by postmodernist antinarratives with their goodbyes to all that.

We find ourselves, therefore, with a plurality of interpretations of Exodus. We find ourselves with diverse religious classics among many religious traditions. We find ourselves glimpsing the plurality within each tradition of interpretation while also admitting the ambiguity of every interpretation: liberating possibilities to be retrieved, errors to be criticized, unconscious distortions to be unmasked.

The attempt to understand remains an effort to interpret well. But to interpret as pluralistic, ambiguous, and important a phenomenon as the paradigm of Exodus is to enter a conflict of interpretations from which there can often seem no exit. The conflicts on how to interpret any religious classic, the conflicts caused by the opposing claims of the religions themselves, and the internal conflicts within any great religion, these all affect interpreters whether they will it or not. None of these conflicts is easily resolved, and no claim to certainty, whether religionist or secularist, should pretend otherwise.

We can continue to give ourselves over to the great hope of Western reason, including the hope for adequate interpretation. But that hope is now a more modest one as a result of the discovery of the plurality of both language and knowledge and the ambiguities of all histories, including the history of reason itself. And yet that hope of reason — a hope expressed, for Westerners, in the models of conversation, argument, and interpretation first created by the Greeks — still lives through any honest fidelity to the classic Socratic imperative: "The unreflective life is not worth living."

We can continue to give ourselves over to the great hope alive in the Exodus narrative: a trust in God as acting for the total liberation of humankind, a hope for our free ability to resist what must be resisted; a hope, if necessary, in hope itself; a hope that, like Exodus, fights against many postmodern exhausted notions of what hope might be. For most religious believers, that Exodus hope arises from the belief that God is grace-ful and will enter into covenant with an empowered, transformed people who will struggle for freedom and liberation. For secular interpreters of Exodus that hope may be glimpsed in the text by sensing some enlightenment, however tentative, and some utopian possibility of emancipation, however modest — as Ernst Bloch taught all to do anew with the text of Exodus and the prophets.

As for the rest, there is no release for any of us from the conflict of interpretations on this central symbol of Exodus if we would understand Judaism or Christianity or Western culture at all. The alternative is not an escape into the transient pleasures of irony, or a flight into despair and cynicism or more history-as-usual. The alternative is not a new kind of innocence or a passivity masking apathy. What Exodus teaches everyone includes this: Whoever fights for hope, fights on behalf of us all; whoever acts on that hope in concrete historical and political struggle, acts in a manner worthy of a human being. And whoever so acts, acts in a manner faintly suggestive of the reality and power of that God in whose image human beings were formed to resist, to think, and to act: that God-of-Exodus who calls oppressed individuals and peoples even now — to struggle, in the wilderness for years if necessary, in firm hope of the promised land ahead.

III. The Interpretation of the Preferred Ones

There are many exemplary scholarly studies of Exodus. But even more than is the case with most religious classics, we also need to hear the interpretations of Exodus by oppressed and marginalized peoples, the "preferred ones" of the God of Exodus.

How those preferred ones read the scriptural texts in their own situation becomes imperative for all interpreters to hear. It was, after all, the black slaves in the American antebellum South, not their white masters, who rightly interpreted the heart of the liberation narrative of Exodus. God's option for the poor is central to the scriptures. This is not to say that option for the poor is translatable into the distinct claim that only the poor can provide proper readings of these texts, any more than it suggests that only the poor can experience revelation or find salvation, or only the poor are the objects of that radical love of neighbor which is the heart of the Christian Gospel. That option does not translate into the position that says, once the poor make their interpretations, all others are to sit back and passively receive them. In that case, are these new and conflictual readings heard at all? Such passive receptions are engendered by conflict, fear, and guilt, not responsibility. They mask a patronizing anxiety that is the forgotten underside of all elite claims to mastery and control.

The option for the poor does translate, however, into the insistence that the readings of the oppressed must be heard, and preferably heard first. In terms of the Scripture's own standards, the oppressed are the ones most likely to hear clearly the full religious and political demands of the prophets. Among our contemporaries their readings are those the rest of us most need to hear. Through their interpretations and actions we can finally read these texts with new eyes and thereby free ourselves from all idealist readings. The mystical-political texts of the prophets and Exodus insist upon both spiritual and material liberation. Recall the prophet's judgments on Israel for its treatment of widows, orphans, and the poor; recall the New Testament's portrayal of Jesus as the friend of the outcasts of his day. Christian salvation is not exhausted by any program of political liberation, to be sure, but Christian salvation, rightly understood, cannot be divorced from the struggle for total human liberation — individual, social, political and religious.

As these new readings by and for the oppressed are heard by all theologians, and in principle by all interpreters of religion, a yet deeper sense of our own plurality and ambiguity will surface and give rise to further conflicts of interpretations over the religious classics like Exodus. Beyond the questions of the sexism, racism, classism, and anti-Semitism in the Jewish and Christian classics and their history of effects upon all interpretations, lies a further disturbing question: is there yet another illusion systemically operative in much theological discourse — the belief, rarely expressed but often acted upon, that only a learned elite can read these texts properly? For these texts are "our" property. All who wish to enter the discussion should leave the "margins" and come to the centers to receive the proper credentials. They must earn property rights if they are to fashion proper readings of the religious classics.

This kind of unconscious elitism, I have come to believe, is not mere error. Like other distortions, elitism is both unconscious and systemic. It is a distortion whose power will be broken only when we learn to hear the alternative readings of the oppressed. The most powerful acts of resistance are often those where the first lesson is to resist oneself. Many theologians have begun to learn that lesson on racism, sexism, classism, and anti-Semitism. It is time to learn the same kind of lesson on elitism. Exodus can teach us all that anew, especially the interpretations of Exodus by the poor throughout history. The academic theologian, like all postmodern intellectuals, needs to learn better ways to hear these new voices. Through attending to the readings and actions by the oppressed of Exodus, we too may learn to become, not alienated egos, but human subjects in active solidarity with all those others we have too often presumed to speak for: that, too, is part of the great narrative of Exodus.

7

Cosmology and Christian Hope

I. The Changed Situation in Theory and Praxis

A return to the issues of cosmology seems both desirable and necessary in our present theological situation. That return is desirable largely because of significant shifts in the methods and contents of both theology and science. The return is necessary for two related reasons. First, there is a growing sense (occasioned by the ecological crisis and the threat of nuclear holocaust) that the "anthropocentric" character of much contemporary theology must be challenged. Second, redemption itself cannot be understood without a relationship to creation; history cannot be understood without nature; the central categories of God and the self (and, therefore, society and history) cannot be fully grasped without reference to the category "cosmos" or "world." Above all, it is the new *status quaestionis* that must be understood before any new constructive theological work can be assessed.

Our contemporary theological situation, to repeat, has changed in both theory and praxis. In both cases, the urgency of a theological return to cosmological interests seems clear. Consider, first, the situation from the point of view of contemporary theory. We forget all too easily that when theologians of early modernity (seventeenth century to early twentieth century) approached the relationships between science and theology the situation was, at best, deeply troubling. The scientific revolution was an intellectual event, as Butter-

This article originally appeared as an editorial in *Concilium* 1983/6. It was coauthored with Nicholas Lash, although only the part written by David Tracy is included here. The entire article, however, was written in consultation with Nicholas Lash.

field remarks, that became a genuine intellectual revolution demanding a new "thinking cap" in all disciplines. Indeed, so radical was this intellectual revolution that Butterfield does not exaggerate when he states that, in comparison, even the Renaissance and the Reformation look like "family quarrels." There can be little doubt that the events symbolized by the names Copernicus, Galileo, Newton, and Darwin changed forever the landscape of theological thought.

Neither the earlier "warfare" between science and religion nor earlier "concordist" proposals of theologians and philosophers in that long period of early modernity strikes contemporaries as genuine options for our radically changed situation. The principal reasons for the collapse of both the confrontational ("warfare") model and the concordist model are to be found in the changed understandings of the content and the methods of both theology and science. For however alive earlier scientific models of mechanism, materialism, and positivism may be in the popular imagination (including the popular imagination of some scientists), the fact is that science itself has challenged the intellectual pretensions of these earlier models. It is not possible in an age where the content of science has been radically changed by evolutionary theories, relativity, quantum mechanics, the principle of indeterminacy, quarks, DNA research, etc., simply to appeal to earlier mechanist or materialist models. The content of the sciences now disallows all easy appeals to these positions. In an ironic symbol of this momentous shift, we may say that science itself no longer has need of Laplace's materialist and mechanist hypothesis! The methods of science, moreover, have themselves yielded to more modest self-appraisals. The recognition that reason too has a history has yielded, in the history of science, to proposals like those of Thomas Kuhn, Stephen Toulmin, M. Hesse, and others that earlier positivist models for scientific self-understanding cannot survive the study of the history of science nor philosophical scrutiny by philosophers of science.

This shift in both the content and the self-understanding of the methods of science has occasioned, therefore, a new intellectual situation where the relationship of science and theology seems at once more promising and more difficult. It is more difficult in the properly theoretical sense that the issues are now far more complex and often highly technical: for this reason alone earlier models of sheer confrontation or easy concordism are inappropriate. It is more promising because the collapse of earlier mechanistic, materialist, and positivist models has freed science itself to a sense of the ultimate mystery of reality and to a chastened but real willingness to dialogue with any plausible philosophical and theological cosmological hypotheses. The dialogue with process philosophers and theologians (including, in the wider sense of process thought, the followers of Teilhard de Chardin) is merely one well-known instance of this increasingly fruitful relationship.

It is equally important to recall, of course, that theological self-understanding and theological content have undergone analogous paradigm shifts in the same period. Except for fundamentalists, earlier theological models based on ahistorical and authoritarian understandings of theological claims have collapsed. Except for naive concordists, the technical complexities and tentative, hypothetical character of the theologically relevant issues in contemporary science do not lend themselves to easy solutions. Indeed, all easy solutions — scientific and theological — have been unmasked as, in effect, ideologies for intellectual elites functioning to assure the *status quo*.

Theologians, in sum, have learned their own form of chastened methodological and material modesty. Most now realize, as Edward Schillebeeckx has observed, that theology is an interpretive enterprise that attempts to establish "mutually critical correlations" (in both theory and praxis) between interpretations of our contemporary situation and interpretations of the Christian tradition. The rise of historical consciousness in the nineteenth century and the radical sense of historicity in the early twentieth century have impelled modern theology, as Bernard Lonergan observed, to abandon its commitments to "classical consciousness" (including classical cosmologies). Granted these gains, one still cannot avoid the impression that (with some notable exceptions) contemporary theology, although strong on interpretations of history and redemption, is relatively weak on interpretations of nature and creation. Part of the reason for this is undoubtedly that earlier "warfares" between science and theology and the collapse of earlier concordist proposals have rendered most theologians reluctant to reenter the dialogue with natural science. The fact that most theologians, by both predilection and training, find their most natural "conversation partners" in the human sciences has also served to encourage this same development. An allied fact is that the major gain of contemporary theology is the "deprivatizing" of theology. This deprivatizing has been best developed by political and liberation theologies faithful to a practical reason cognizant of massive global suffering. Yet, those very same theologies can often encourage a relative lack of interest in strictly cosmological questions.

It should now be clear, especially to readers of *Concilium,* that a major accomplishment and a still major need of contemporary theology is to work out political and liberation theologies faithful to the demands of both theory and praxis in our grave historical situation. These theologies correctly retrieve the resources of the Christian tradition to help transform that situation of massive global suffering. Their critical analysis of the complicity in "privatization" on the part of earlier modern existentialist and transcendental theologies can only be considered a gain for all theology. The suspicion that "cosmological" interests in theology *can* function as a distraction from these historical responsibilities or even as ideology for intellectual elites (as in concordist proposals) seems, admittedly, in order. The importance of these suspicions should not be domesticated. Indeed, any pure models of "progress" unable and unwilling to face the tragedy and suffering in human existence fully deserve Christian theological suspicion, indeed contempt.

Yet another suspicion must also inform our contemporary theological consciousness: is it possible for theology to be faithful to the demands of either our situation or the Christian tradition while continuing to ignore cosmological concerns? The question is not merely rhetorical. For the fact is that the rediscovery of "history" by contemporary theology has not been matched by a parallel rediscovery of "nature." A well-nigh exclusive focus on the doctrine of redemption (as related to liberation and emancipation) has not been paralleled by new explorations of the doctrine of creation. Contemporary theology is in danger of developing interpretations of God and self (including the social self in society and history) while quietly dropping the traditional third category of "world" or "cosmos." And yet this absence would represent a major impoverishment of the Christian tradition and possibly a major distortion of Christian understandings of salvation and history by themselves.

It is, of course, necessary to continue to demythologize and de-ideologize traditional Christian theological understandings of "world" or "cosmos." Nevertheless, it is also crucial to realize that, from the New Testament period through the patristic and the medieval periods, the same insight has prevailed. In J. Collins's forthright statement:

> Human salvation cannot be divorced from our understanding of the world around us. The creation, too, is groaning in travail. . . .
> It is important . . . that we find a way to integrate human values

with some cosmological understanding if our theology is to represent more than a fragment of existence.

The Christian tradition needs the doctrine of creation even to understand fully its own doctrine of redemption. Contemporary Christian theology needs to recover a theology of nature — even to develop an adequate theology of history. No Christian theology can claim adequacy to the Christian tradition by, in effect, retrieving only God and the self (including the social and historical self) while quietly dropping "world" out of the picture. The questions of cosmology are not properly understood as *only* concerned with the origin and natural structure of the world. Those cosmological questions include the destiny of the world, as well — including the destiny of human beings, indeed of history itself — as "inextricably bound up" with the destiny of the cosmos. The deprivatizing of theology has meant a return to real history (not merely historicity). But that return to history, in both theory and praxis, must also mean a return to nature.

These more theoretical questions, moreover, are intensified if we note two central practical concerns of our contemporary period. Those two grave issues — in summary form, the ecological crisis and the threat of nuclear holocaust — must touch all contemporary theologies of history. Both issues, moreover, suggest in graphic terms all more theoretical questions. For the relationships between science and religion today are not occasioned only by the intriguing and complex set of intellectual issues posed by the new paradigms for method in science and theology and the new content in both disciplines. Nor is the need for cosmology in theology, posed only by the internal theological demands that theology attempt to interpret both self and world in light of its Christic understanding of God; that theology interpret creation even to understand redemption; that theology risk interpreting nature in order to understand history. Central and pressing as these intellectual concerns undoubtedly are, they, too, must be understood in the context of our contemporary, realistic sense of genuine crisis. The reality of impending ecological crisis is so clear that no serious concern with historical justice can long ignore it. The struggle for justice must also include the struggle for ecology — not only to secure justice for other creatures than the human, but even to secure the most basic justice of all: a livable environment for future generations of human beings. The ecological crisis forces all serious political and liberation theology to call into question, on its own praxis criteria, the possible anthropocentrism lurking in its self-understanding.

As John Cobb suggests, all cosmologically-informed theologies (like Cobb's own process theology) must now be in conversation with political and liberation theologians in order to become a political theology. It is also the case that all political and liberation theology must now become an ecological theology as well in order to fulfill its own demands to relate to our present praxis situation. This means that a reopening of cosmological concerns in contemporary theology will also become a dialogue between political theology and those forms of "postmodern" ecological science (Stephen Toulmin, Frederick Ferré) whose own praxis concerns are clear. All must now share a critique and suspicion of traditional scientific and theological understandings of the human right to "dominate" and exploit nature.

Allied to this sense of concern for the ecological crisis is, of course, the other central praxis issue which our contemporary situation poses: the threat of omnicide present in the possibility of nuclear holocaust. The concern among scientists and theologians alike with this central dilemma imposes, besides its more obvious political implications, a need to interpret cosmology anew. Such interpretations may help to avert this overwhelming and literally final nuclear possibility for the entire planet. The issues — technical, political, and cosmological as well as theological — involved in both ecology and the possibility of nuclear war are so pressing that only a collaborative effort among all persons "of good will" (including scientists and theologians) can hope to find ways — in theory and praxis — to avert the crisis. For the moment, our point is a more simple and more basic one: viz. that it is now impossible for theology to understand itself as responding to the theoretical and practical challenges of our situation while ignoring the issues of cosmology. If theology is to remain a discipline establishing mutually critical correlations in theory and praxis between interpretations of the situation and interpretations of the tradition, then cosmology must once again be accorded a central place in all theological reflection. Otherwise, we would not be faithful to either the demands of the new intellectual situation in both science and theology nor the crises in praxis which impinge on us all. Nor could we claim, under the rubric of a theology of history, that we have adequately interpreted the full resources and demands of the Christian tradition itself; redemption *and* creation; history *and* nature; God, self, *and* world. Thus the challenge to all theology: a challenge to recognize the new *status quaestionis* which our contemporary situation poses; a challenge to allow, indeed demand that cosmological concerns reenter all contemporary theology. Both the earlier "warfare" between science and religion and all concordist resolutions are clearly spent. The demand is rather for a collaboration effort that can help establish plausible "mutually critical correlations" not only to interpret our world but to help it.

II. Nature, History, and Hope

The dialogue between contemporary political and liberation theologies of history and cosmological theologies in our period could begin with joint reflection on a central category of the Christian theology of history itself: the category of hope. The rediscovery of the prophetic, eschatological, and apocalyptic traditions as bearing political resources could also occasion a retrieval of the cosmic hope present in the wisdom (and cosmological) dimensions of those same traditions. Indeed, in terms of a properly negative function, the theological category of hope challenges both historical ideologies of Western evolutionary liberal progress as well as all cosmologies of progress (whether naturalist-materialist or religious). Both the prophetic and the wisdom traditions recognize what ideologies of progress cannot see: the stark reality of radical evil, tragedy, and sin in all existence and the need for concrete and realistic actions against those evils — action grounded in a fundamental trust — hope in the God of history and nature alike.

There is no possibility in our period for a single, all-embracing "scientific" cosmological narrative. There is also no possibility, on the theological side, for a complete system of final understanding of God-self-world. What there is, however, is an envisionment of reality informed by the hope afforded by the Christian construal of all reality from the perspective of Jesus Christ. In classical ages where a finite, closed, and seemingly perfectly ordered cosmos seemed plausible, that Christian construal could focus on the incarnation as the always-already immanent and transcendent reality of God's presence to world, self, and history. In our present age all purely incarnational cosmic theologies do not seem a live option. For we have moved from the closed world to an infinite universe (A. Koyré). We now recognize more fully the tragic and radical evil in our midst. We fear with reason for the fate of all humanity, indeed of the entire planet in the shadow of massive global suffering and the threats of ecological crisis and nuclear holocaust.

It is not the case, of course, that Christians have ceased to believe in the incarnation of Jesus Christ. It is the case that Christians now recognize that the incarnation itself can only be properly interpreted in the light of the ministry, cross, and resurrection of Jesus Christ. That ministry stands as a stark call to a life of Christian discipleship modeled on the praxis of radically evangelical *imitatio Christi*. The cross intrudes upon all optimism as a stark reminder of the not-yet, the suffering and tragedy at the heart of all existence. The resurrection discloses the reality of Christian hope for nature and history alike as proleptically present in God's vindication of the ministry and cross of Jesus Christ.

It is, therefore, Jesus Christ who continues to provide the decisive clue for a Christian envisionment of God, world, and self, of nature and history, creation and redemption. Yet that theological vision is now recognized to include not only the always-ready reality of the incarnation but also the not-yet realities manifested in the ministry and the cross and the hope for all history and nature disclosed in the resurrection. It is the stark dialectic of this always/already/not-yet Christic actuality which can inform all Christian theological construals of God, self, and world. Insofar as Christian theology is the establishment of mutually critical correlations between situation and tradition, this means that theological work must be collaborative with all disciplines competent to interpret both the self (the human sciences including philosophy) and the world (the natural sciences, including philosophy of science and cosmology). Insofar as Christian theology is also Christian this means that the incarnation-ministry-cross-resurrection of Jesus Christ will remain the classic Christian clue to an environment of God, self and world in critical correlation with modern theories and contemporary demands of praxis.

The radical theocentrism that should inform all theology as *theologia* means, for Christian theology, that self and world will be understood in the light of God. It means as well that the singular, decisive clue to God's own reality and to the realities of self and world (history and nature, redemption and creation) will be understood in relationship to the God disclosed in Jesus Christ. As this Christic reality becomes more and more recognized as the center of theologies of history and nature alike — as the always/already/not-yet reality it is — then the Christian theological category of *hope* will become more and more prominent. For it is theological hope which is likely to become as important in theologies of nature as in theologies of history. Christian hope, focused upon this always/already/not-yet reality of Jesus Christ, unmasks historical and cosmic optimism and pessimism alike as unacceptable to Christian faith. The fact is that the easy optimism of earlier concordist cosmologies crashed against the reality of tragedy. And every easy pessimism encourages a quietism that crashes against the reality of genuine Christian hope and the actions demanded by that hope.

Neither optimism nor pessimism but hope is at the heart of the Christian vision of both nature and history. That hope not merely allows but demands both theoretical reflection and concrete praxis. Christian hope is grounded in the always/already/not-yet reality of Jesus Christ as a primary theological clue for our new cosmological and historical situation. Insofar as that situation now demands a theology of history *and* nature, a theology of redemption *and* creation, it suggests that all theologians would do well to focus again on that central category of hope. Then we may begin to see more fully — in critical conversation with modern science, history, philosophy and praxis — some fuller reasons for "the hope that lies in us" and the beginnings of a new Christian construal of God, self, and world.

Part Four

Catholic Concerns

8

Roman Catholic Identity amid the Ecumenical Dialogues

I. The Three Elements of Roman Catholic Identity

The important dialogues of Roman Catholics and the other major Christian churches have yielded enormous fruit. Like many theologians, it is my hope that the remarkable theological agreements achieved in true dialogues will be accepted throughout the Christian churches. Any agreement based upon the kind of theological care and acuteness in those dialogues deserves not merely the encouragement but the strong endorsement of all serious ecumenical Christians. It is dialogue with others, moreover, which helps any careful thinker to rediscover one's own identity. Sometimes, indeed, only such dialogue can help one discover that identity — as if for the first time.

Rather than attending to the many important and well-known specific theological, doctrinal, and church order issues resulting from the dialogues, this article will step back to observe the more general question of Roman Catholic identity in the midst of these ecumenical dialogues. To achieve this more general aim, the analysis will take the following form: first a return to two modern Catholic and ecumenical thinkers — John Henry Cardinal Newman and Baron Friedrich von Hügel — for their classic analyses of the fuller complexity of the question of Roman Catholic identity; second some further reflections informed by contemporary ecumenical dialogues on each of the three

Source: *Concilium* 1994/5, *Catholic Identity*, edited by James H. Provost and Knut Walf.

components (the institutional, the intellectual, and the life of piety) constituting Roman Catholic identity as Catholic.[1]

Newman's reflections on the reality of the church bear a distinctly Catholic mark. When Newman appealed to the "idea" of the church, he understood "idea" as one's deepest sense of the concrete whole and its constituent parts at once. Like so many in his age, "idea" meant to Newman not an abstraction from reality but reality itself as spiritually sensed and partially but never fully understood. In his *Essay on the Development of Doctrine* Christianity was such an organic idea: sensed, felt, understood, and yielding itself to partial, incomplete, but true understanding as it developed through the centuries. The church, as an idea, was the objective reality of the Body of Christ, constituted by the Spirit of Christ. That is why only the truly spiritual could understand the church and why the Christian experienced and understood Christ and the Spirit in and through the church.

The idea of the church was never for Newman a mere idea but the polity which is the church existing here and now: the one Catholics live in, whose gifted reality, as well as human faults and need for self-reform, is always there. It is a part, therefore, of Catholic spirituality to sense and understand the church in its unity and in its distinct parts — parts that can never efface the antecedent divinely graced unity. It is also part of Catholic spirituality to struggle to discern what part of the church now needs strengthening, or development, or correction of excesses by reform. The temptation of the prophetical teaching office (theology) is rationalism; that of the ruling office is power; that of the sacred ministry and piety is superstition. Each temptation needs to be discerned and healed, and the danger of each part thinking itself the whole church needs to be avoided. Thus could Newman appeal to history when, in the fourth century, most of the bishops abandoned the true christological doctrine in the Arian controversy and the church depended on the laity to maintain its true identity. This example impelled Newman to insist on the need to consult the laity and to defend the *sensus fidelium* as a truly ecclesial sense.

In sum, for Newman doctrine, sacrament, tradition, community, and above all church as Body of Christ comprising three equally indispensable functions form the spirituality of Catholics in all cultures. This formation allows a great diversity of spiritual ways while uniting them in the central reality of the Spirit's indwelling presence to the individual soul in communion with church as the spiritual presence of Christ. Newman's exceptional sensitivity to the need for diversity and powers of discernment in the ever-shifting historical and theological reality of the church made his spirituality influential for many modern Catholics as both unmistakably Catholic and clearly modern. That same spiritual sense pervades the openness to the good in other religious traditions and to the best of modernity in the major decrees of the Second Vatican Council and the recent ecumenical dialogues.

One major example of the influence of Newman on his younger contemporaries may be found in the thought of Baron Friedrich von Hügel.[2] Although perhaps mostly remembered for his complex role in the modernist crises of the early twentieth century, Baron von Hügel's contribution to modern Catholic spirituality is best found in his classic work, *The Mystical Element of Religion as Studied in Saint Catherine of Genoa and Her Friends.*

Von Hügel's own work may be viewed as a further modern development of Newman's insight into Catholic diversity-in-unity. Von Hügel applied that Newmanian insight not solely to the reality of the church but to the reality of religion itself. Von Hügel was far less theological than Newman and less concerned, therefore, with showing the theological reality of the church as the presence of Christ's indwelling Spirit. His principal concern was to develop a philosophy of religion that could show the actuality of the concrete person as a unity-in-diversity and thereby the actuality of religion as having the character of a concrete person with both great multiplicity and real unity.

Philosophically, von Hügel (in harmony with the radical empiricism and personalism of his period) developed a personalist philosophy that argued for the presence of emotional, intellectual, and volitional elements acting in harmony in every person. He believed, as did Coleridge and Newman before him, that a prior unity is given to any concrete personal reality. That reality can be sensed and lived but never fully analyzed. One can, however, note the need for the complex development of each person for the full development and harmonization of the emotional, intellectual, and volitional elements.

This personalist model deeply informs von Hügel's discussion of religion in *The Mystical Element of Religion.* There he attempts to show, on the occasion of a historical study of the action-in-the-everyday spirituality of St. Catherine of Genoa, that every living religion bears its clearest analogue in the living person. The believer knows and trusts the concrete reality of God disclosed in the religion. As with a person, the living unity and trust are concretely realized before analysis and criticism are forthcoming. Analogous to the emotional, intellectual, and volitional elements in the person, religion exercises three principal functions. It continuously needs to develop each element and its interrelationships to the other elements to achieve the balance and harmony of an authentic personality.

This personalist analogy led von Hügel to his promising suggestion for understanding the three major elements comprising a historical religion. He employed various phrases for this distinction. One of them insists that every concrete religion comprises three elements: (1) "the external, authoritative, historical, traditional, and institutional element" (analogous to the volitional elements in the person); (2) "the critical-historical and synthetic-philosophical element" (analogous to the intellectual); and (3) "the mystical and directly operative element of religion" (analogous to the emotional).

Von Hügel attempted, above all, to be faithful to the complexity of Catholic Christianity while also attending to some peculiarly modern intellectual needs. Examples of von Hügel's combination of Catholic balance and modernity are seen in the following: (1) the "institutional" element is real and to be affirmed, but only as related to the necessary fullness of this "external" element more fully described as authoritative, historical, and traditional; (2) the "intellectual" element is crucial and now, in the modern period, must include not only the philosophical-synthetic (as in the classic scholastic theologies and their less happy — for von Hügel — neo-scholastic successors) but also the critical-historical (as in biblical and doctrinal studies); (3) the "mystical" element is not merely passive, but includes a note of action as well — as the spirituality of Catherine of Genoa shows; as, indeed, for von Hügel the most representatively Catholic mystical spiritualities (as incarnational) are also action-oriented in principle.

What Newman attempted to show under the theological rubric of "church," von Hügel addressed under the philosophical rubric of "religion." Both can be considered classic modern reflections on Catholic identity in an ecumenical setting. Both insist that God's reality is mediated in the concrete historical form of church (Newman) and religion (von Hügel). Only attention to that concreteness as sensed by the believer assures both the personalism and the objectivity essential in Catholic identity. Both acknowledge that this unity occurred in great spiritual diversity: a diversity occasioned by different temperaments, cultures, and historical periods and a diversity grounded in the triple office of the church (Newman) or the threefold elements of concrete religion (von Hügel). Both insisted that in Catholic identity this sense of God's reality is mediated to us in Jesus Christ and the church. Both also insisted on the constant spiritual need for Catholics to discern critically corrections and developments of these three functions as well as the contributions and promise of modernity for Catholic self-understanding.

II. The Three Elements of Roman Catholic Identity and Their Continuing Reform

Since the renewal of the church's spirit and structures in the Second Vatican Council, several new images and models have been used to express further these insights on Catholicism and its identity.[3] First, consider the institutional element in the midst of the new images for church. What first strikes any observer of the Catholic church is the phenomenon of its sheer "lasting-power" and size as an institution. The model or image of the church as institution is both true to the fact of the church's historical life and an authentic model or image for many important aspects of that life. Viewing the church as institution, one can understand its social reality and its use of various institutional forms in various periods of history; for example, the church's use of corporation theory in the medieval period; the use of the "perfect society" model in the Tridentine period; and the use of the model of collegiality in Vatican II. The effectiveness of the church's transnational commitment to social justice in the world, for example, continues to depend largely upon its ability to remain a cohesive and vital institution that witnesses a common spirit for justice. The effectiveness of its commitment to its own internal reform also depends upon continued incorporation of its own collegiality model into its internal institutional forms. The institutional model remains, therefore, a vital factor in the church's self-understanding. Its continuing reform remains urgent, as the ecumenical dialogues clearly show.

Four other models employed since Vatican II have proved especially helpful in highlighting various aspects of the church's life. They are: the church as mystical communion; as sacrament; as herald; and as servant and prophet. When one speaks of the church as "mystical communion" one means to affirm that the church is and will always remain not merely a human institution but a mystery as profound as all the other central mysteries of God's self-revelation in Jesus Christ. The social reality of the church is also the social reality of a common

union (a "communion") grounded in the mystery of God's action in
Jesus. Following St. Paul, the church uses the image of the mystical
body to describe this social reality of ecclesial union in and with
Christ. Again following the Scriptures, the Second Vatican Council
helped Catholics realize that reality more deeply by proclaiming the
liberating image of the church as the people of God. These images
alert one, as institutional language alone cannot, to the fact that the
church is ultimately a mystery grounded in Jesus Christ enlivened by
his Spirit. As Newman and von Hügel insisted, therein lies a
grounded Catholic identity.

The image or model of the church as sacrament of the encounter
with God allows one to unify the insights of the first two models. To
speak of the church as "sacrament" suggests both its incarnate and
institutional reality and its mysterious reality as Christ's presence in
the world. By using the model or image of "herald," the church
wishes to emphasize its character as an event: as the actual congrega-
tion of those faithful to God's word, gathered together by the
preached word itself. The church is never more the church than when
gathered together at the eucharist to hear God's word and celebrate
the sacraments in each local church. The recent emphasis upon the
Church as herald of the good news of the gospel and upon the "local
church" (possibly inspired by the dialogues) is a striking reminder
that no matter how wide the vision, nor how universal the commitments, the church is in the first place "church" in the local community where the eucharist and word are celebrated.

Each model or image allows for another and distinctive glimpse
into the reality of the church. In affirming the church as institution
Catholics affirm its social reality and effectiveness. In affirming the
church as mystical body and people of God they affirm that their
deepest union as a people is communion in the radical mystery of
God's gift in Jesus Christ. In affirming the church as sacrament
Catholics recall how the church makes present anew that mystery in
words, actions, symbols, and sacraments. In affirming the church as
herald of the gospel they recall how the experience of the church is
rooted in — indeed incarnate in — the local church's fidelity to the
gospel and celebration of the eucharist.

But not even all these rich images and models for understanding
the church exhaust its reality. The church in the modern world has
also emphasized its role as servant to humanity and prophet to humanity. As the great liberation movements around the world have
shown, the church is also the servant of humanity, especially of the

poor and the oppressed, and should be prophetic concerning the real needs of the day. The model or image of the servant church reminds Catholics that the church is not closed in upon itself, not called to a triumphalism over the world. Rather the church as church, in fidelity to Jesus Christ as the Suffering Servant, is called to turn out toward the world and to suffer for and with the poor and the oppressed.

The image or model of the church as a prophetic witness to humanity recalls that the church has the authentic vocation of the prophets of the Old Testament. In fidelity to Jesus Christ, the church is not called simply to applaud the powers that reign nor to bless the *status quo*. Rather, it should also perform a critical and prophetic function. By employing the rich religious resources of the Old and New Testament prophetic traditions and the resources from faith and reason of its own tradition of social justice, the church must speak to the world in judgment upon all these principalities and powers — economic, social, cultural, and political — which aid any form of oppression, by understanding itself as servant church and prophetic witness, the church declares that Catholics are all called to the struggle for justice, not as an extra avocation but as the concrete embodiment of the church's true vocation as servant to humanity.

The church's struggle for justice also involves the creation of just structures and the performance of just actions within the church itself as the ecumenical dialogues also help to clarify. As the *ecclesia semper reformanda*, the church always in need of reform, it must be constantly aware of the need to assure just practices and procedures within its own institutional forms. The central principles of the Catholic tradition of social justice — the dignity of every person, the importance of assuring economic, cultural, social, and political equality of opportunity for all, the joint principles of subsidiarity and the common good — should be embodied in institutional reforms of the church's internal practices.

The reforms of the institutional elements of the Roman Catholic tradition continue to need constant attention. The theological contributions to that institutional reform (including the implicit contribution from the ecumenical dialogues) are genuine — as the analysis of the influence of different theological models for church already suggests. However, the other two "elements" of Catholic identity (the intellectual and the life of piety or spirituality) also need further reflection.

In the Catholic tradition, part of Catholic intellectual identity is the close relationship between theology and philosophy (and, therefore, between "faith" and "reason"). It is difficult to conceive of a strictly Roman Catholic Barthian position. Even the closest contemporary analogue to Barth in Roman Catholic theology, Hans Urs von Balthasar, remains notably Catholic in appeals to philosophy in theology and in his brilliant defenses of analogy, aesthetics, and form in theology. This insight can lead one to the following generalization: a part of Catholic theological identity is some sense of an affirmation of "reason" (and thereby philosophy or the philosophical side of the other disciplines) for use in theology. The relationships between theology and philosophy in Catholic identity cover a wide spectrum indeed; but rarely is the position simply confrontational as in Karl Barth or simply dismissive of "metaphysics" and "mysticism" as in so many neo-orthodox and even some liberal Protestant (Albert Ritschl) theologians.

One of the singular events of the last fifteen years, moreover, is the closer relationship of the "intellectual" and "spiritual" elements in Catholic identity: consider, for example, the new relationship developed between Catholic theology and spirituality. Indeed, it is now widely agreed that a distinction between theology and spirituality (unlike the distinction between theology and philosophy) was allowed to become a separation. That separation of theology and spirituality has proved disastrous to both. Once separated from spirituality, theology is in danger of becoming merely abstract. Theology then begins to offer stones where all want bread. Once separated from theology, spirituality is always in danger of becoming merely sentimental. Spirituality begins to offer cake when people demand bread.

The many attempts to reunite Catholic theology and spirituality (and thereby the "intellectual" and "spiritual" elements of Catholic identity), especially those influenced by the ecumenical dialogues, has proved crucial for Roman Catholic identity. This has occurred in two principal ways. First, the traditional Catholic emphasis on sacrament (indeed its sacramental envisionment of all reality) continues as central to any Catholic identity. Now, however, thanks partly to the Roman Catholic-ecumenical dialogues, it is more accurate to speak of the word-sacrament dialectic in Catholic identity. In a similar way, the traditional Catholic theological commitment to an analogical imagination and language (which are, after all, the direct conceptual counterpart of a Catholic religious sacramental vision) now also possess more dialectical moments, again thanks partly to the ecumenical dialogues.

Secondly, these dialogues have also encouraged the development of new forms of what Gustavo Gutiérrez and others have named a "mystical-political" spirituality and theology.[4] These political, liberation, and feminist theologies have reunited not only theory and praxis but theology and spirituality — and often in an ecumenical manner. Roman Catholic identity is now far more complex and pluralistic than in the past but remains recognizably Catholic. Newman and von Hügel could acknowledge the greater ecumenical diversity in the new forms of unity-in-diversity of a new Catholic identity. The future for Roman Catholic identity remains as promising as its willingness to enrich the institutional, spiritual, and intellectual elements in an ever new unity-in-diversity. No small part of that newly emergent Roman Catholic identity will be played by a fuller incorporation of the ecumenical dialogues into further institutional reform, deeper spiritual enrichment, and a firmer ecumenical character for all Catholic theology. Surely Roman Catholic identity as both fundamentally Catholic and genuinely — i.e., inclusively — catholic can welcome this.

NOTES

1. I have developed this analysis of Newman and von Hügel further for the question of the unity-in-diversity of Roman Catholic spirituality in "Recent Catholic Spirituality: Unity amid Diversity," in Louis Dupré and Don E. Saliers (eds.), *Christian Spirituality III: Post-Reformation and Modern* (New York and London 1989). For the fuller analysis see that article.

2. On von Hügel, see *The Mystical Element of Religion as Studied in St. Catherine of Genoa and Her Friends* (2 vols.) (London 1908).

3. See Avery Dulles, *Models of the Church* (New York 1976).

4. Inter alia, see Gustavo Gutiérrez, *On Job: God-Talk and the Suffering of the Innocent* (Maryknoll, New York 1984).

9

The Catholic Model of *Caritas*

Self-Transcendence and Transformation

I. Some General Definitions

In the theological literature, Catholic and Protestant, there are some standard terms which are employed. Since I use these terms throughout this essay, it may prove helpful to provide some initial definitions of the terms at the beginning. The bibliographic materials (especially Outka) also provide further resources (e.g., D'Arcy, von Balthasar) worth noting. The definitions (which are my own reformulations from the literature) are:

Agape — the gift of God's love in Jesus Christ: it is given; not our achievement — but pure gift, sheer grace which ennobles, empowers, elicits Christians to love God and neighbor in the self-sacrificial manner that God has first loved us in Jesus Christ.

Eros — human striving, yearning of a self for some ideal of happiness as concretely experienced in all concrete human loves; classically expressed in Plato; reformulated in almost every age in accordance with some reigning paradigm of what constitutes authentic human love.

Libido — the pure desire aspect of *eros* abstracted from the self's conscious ideal of happiness. Since Freud, often identified with powerful sexual drive.

Philia — friendship-love; the love of the other as related to the self

Source: *Concilium* 1979/1 (No. 121), *The Family in Crisis or in Transition*, edited by Andrew Greeley.

and the self's own desires, attachments, ideals (related to but not identical with neighbor-love).

Caritas (charity) — since Augustine, the reigning Catholic model: a proposal for a synthesis of human *eros* in the self and the divine *agape* given in Jesus Christ. The particular understandings of both *eros* and *agape* change from one Catholic theologian to another. In every case, however, some synthesis will be formulated; more specifically some transformation of human *eros* (which is basically affirmed) by divine *agape* will be explicated to disclose the concrete and complex experiential reality of *caritas* in Christian lives.

Nomos — love's expression through a fulfillment of law. Often (mistakenly) thought by Christians to represent Judaism's notion of love; genuinely representative, however, of the role of law as an expression of the love of God in both Judaism or Christianity.

It is important to note that these definitions represent my own attempts to achieve a relative consensus on factors debated in the literature. Each definition, for example, is distinct from the famous definitions (especially of *agape* and *eros*) delineated by Anders Nygren in his ground-breaking work *Agape and Eros*.

II. Theology and the Task of Correlation on the Reality of Christian Love

In general terms, Christian theology is a discipline that attempts to correlate the meaning and truth of the Christian fact (its scriptures, doctrines, rituals, witnesses, symbols, etc.) with the meaning and truth of our contemporary experience. When the theologian is principally engaged in one of the three major disciplines within theology (viz. fundamental, systematic, and practical theologies), this fact ordinarily influences the *emphasis* which either side of the correlation will receive. However, every theologian will in fact be involved in some form of correlation of these two realities.

The more explicit form of a model for that procedure of correlation can take several forms. The strictly logical possibilities for correlation can map the three major models actually employed in the history of Christian theology. The most basic logical differences are those among three options: "all," "some" and "none." In theological models these logical options for correlating Christian and secular experience become models of identity (all), confrontation (none), and transformation (some).

1. *Confrontation*: This position holds that there is no correlation between our ordinary human loves (friendship, romantic love, various forms of intimacy, etc.) and the divine love given to us in Jesus Christ. This model is more exactly described as a model of *confrontation* between our ordinary experience and the pure gift of God's revelation. In more general terms, this option is expressed clearly in the famous rhetorical question of Tertullian, "What has Athens to do with Jerusalem?" On the question of love, it is most clearly expressed in Nygren's interpretation of Luther and Paul whereby only the gift of *agape* is Christian love. That gift must *never* be confused with, synthesized with, or even really correlated with the various forms of human striving which constitute *eros*-love in all its modalities. The correlation is paradoxically that there is *no* correlation between *agape* and any form of *eros*; a refusal to face that confrontational reality is, on Nygren's reading, a betrayal of the Christian understanding of *agape*-love by reducing it to some reigning form of *eros*-love.

2. *Identity*: This position holds that there is a complete correlation between Christian agapic love and the love of *eros* in our ordinary experiences of friendship, love, and intimacy. This model for correlation is really one of identity. Ultimately the pure giftedness of any love is identical to the gift of God's love for us in Jesus Christ. Appeals to our common human experiences of intimacy, therefore, would suffice for understanding Christian love. There is ordinarily little recognition of, or at least little accounting for, the actual ambiguity in our human experience of intimacy. Rather the purely positive sides of that experience are highlighted (the creativity, ecstasy, loyalty, and fundamental trust present in all authentic human experiences of love). The "negative" aspects of that experience (the self-aggrandizement, the delusions, the angers and jealousies, the fears and insecurities) are ordinarily either ignored or at least downplayed. Hence Christian love is no more, and no less, than a clearer, a more explicit consciousness of the common human experience of the giftedness, creativity and fundamental trust present in our everyday positive experiences of intimacy and love.

3. *Transformation*: Most theologians develop some explicit transformation model for understanding the correlations between the gift of love in Jesus Christ and our common experience of love. Most contemporary Christian theologians, Catholic and Protestant, in fact employ some particular model of correlation. Indeed the mainline

Catholic theological understanding of the relationships between faith and reason, theology and philosophy, *agape* and *eros* encourages many theologians to believe that the transformation model of correlation is, in fact, the major model for historical and contemporary Catholic theology. On the question of a theological understanding of love, for example, there seems no doubt that the *caritas* tradition present in Catholic Christianity from Augustine to our own day is the paradigm worthy of our communal reflection. Indeed, even before Augustine named *caritas* this attempted synthesis of the pure giftedness of God's agapic love in Jesus Christ with the individual's search for happiness in the legitimate and necessary strivings of authentic *eros*-love, the reality of correlation was present in the Christian tradition. Synthesis was clearly present in the *Logos* theologies of the East: witness Gregory of Nyssa's mystical theology of *eros* and *agape*. The reality of a correlation possibility of synthesis, moreover, is present, in my judgment, in the New Testament itself. Indeed, as Nygren himself admits, it may be found in at least implicit form in the Johannine tradition. Many recent scriptural studies have shown how its presence may be seen in both the synoptics (including — indeed especially — in the parables of Jesus) as well as in the insistence of Paul that Christian love is both gift and command, that Christian love both challenges and fulfills all authentic striving.

In a similar manner, the New Testament challenges any easy identity of Christian love and the "loves" of our common human experience. Indeed God's love for us in Christ Jesus and in the covenant with Israel is always thought of as pure gift, as *grace* which enables, empowers, frees us to love as God has first loved us in Christ Jesus. The pure gift character of authentic Christian love and, in that properly theological sense, the purely agapic graced character of that love is the clear and consistent witness of the entire Christian tradition from the scriptures to the present. Any implicit or explicit *identity* model for the relationships between that love and our common human experience of love must, therefore, show how that common witness can be ignored or retranslated into that alternative of identity (on purely hermeneutical grounds). I do not myself see any way by which an identity model could really account for the pure giftedness, the event-happening-grace character of love present in authentic Christian traditions.

This latter judgment seems even more secure when one recognizes the "extreme" human possibilities of love which the New Testament commands: the love of the enemy; that radical self-sacrificial love decisively represented in the love displayed in the Cross of Christ; the love of every and each neighbor precisely as neighbor (not merely as "friend"). Each of these commands is "extreme" or extraordinary; it is recognized that they do not accord with our ordinary experience of love, fidelity, intimacy, friendship. Indeed, there is profound truth in Friedrich Nietzsche's insistence that New Testament Christianity was, in fact, a revaluation of all ancient values. This is the case because, by its insistence upon real neighbor love — even the love of the enemy and the self-sacrifice of the Cross — Christianity challenged the then reigning paradigm for love, the "friendship" paradigm of the ancient Greeks. Neighbor-love is a command for the Christian, indeed a command to a life at the limits. Yet that command is never simply command, because in Christian self-understanding the Christian is ennobled, empowered, gifted, graced to hear and fulfill that command. Do these scriptural reflections then mean, in effect, that only a confrontation model between Christian *agape* and human *eros* will suffice? As indicated above, a pure confrontation model is itself challenged by both scripture and by the mainline Christian witness — certainly by the Catholic *caritas* model for love. It is necessary, therefore, to provide some further reflections upon the character of a theological transformation model.

It is worth recalling that in the Catholic theological tradition, there are in fact no real major exceptions to the tradition's rejection of both a pure identity and a pure confrontation model. Rather every major Catholic theologian, when reflecting on the reality of love within the Catholic experience, works out a particular transformation model whereby both *agape* and *eros* are correlated into the classical Catholic synthesis of *caritas*. Moreover, there is no doubt that the Catholic *caritas* position on love is not an exception unrelated to other major choices in Catholic theology: a trust in reason along with a religious recognition of the pure giftedness of faith informing various Catholic formulations of the relationships between faith and reason; a religious conviction of the radicality and universality of God's grace informing the classical dictum that grace fulfills but does not destroy nature (including, therefore, *eros*); an anthropology that, while cognizant of the reality of sin in the human condition, tends to emphasize the transformation even of sin by the power of God's grace. Catholic anthropology thereby develops a vision of our common humanity that seems both realistic (on the genuine ambiguity of all human actions) yet optimistic on the ultimate triumph of grace in the human spirit and in history. With Albert Camus, the authentic Catholic sensibility ordinarily believes that "There is more in human beings to admire than to despise." That same sensibility develops an analogical imagination that attempts to order the relationships of God and humankind, nature and history, justice and love, *agape* and *eros* by means of the transformative focal meaning of God's grace in Christ Jesus.

There are almost always major exceptions in the Catholic tradition to at least one of the positions summarized above. The "later" Augustine and Pascal, for example, are in fact less optimistic about the human situation than most Catholic theologians and thereby tend to relate grace to sin more than to nature. And yet even in Augustine and Pascal the final triumph of grace resounds and the *caritas*-synthesis is clearly affirmed. Indeed, from Augustine through Bernard, Aquinas, Bonaventure, Hildegard, Dante, Teresa, Pascal, and Newman to D'Arcy, Scheler, von Balthasar, Stein, Rahner, Lonergan, and Küng, the same leitmotif recurs with different resonances and distinct formulations for the exact character of the transformation: Christian love is best understood on the synthetic and transformative model of *caritas*. Both *agape* and *eros* are to be affirmed and correlated into some higher synthesis to redescribe the human situation and to prescribe those dispositions, habits, and character which are properly "loving."

The exact nature of the correlation of *agape* and *eros* will shift from age to age and even from theologian to theologian in accordance with particular interpretations of both New Testament *agape* and a major contemporary model of *eros*. For example, the individual theologian's "canon within the canon" for understanding New Testament *agape* may be the radically self-sacrificial *kenosis* model of Paul's theology of the Cross. Or that canon may be a Johannine incarnational model that emphasizes the "mutuality" factor in love and the cosmic reality of God's descending love in the *Logos* and human ascending love in the Christian community. Still other theologians may well turn to the parables or the various formulations of the Great Command in the Synoptics to find their major paradigm for love. Then one may well find an emphasis upon the reality of love as both pure gift (in the parables) and radical command (to love God and neighbor). And yet however central a particular paradigm for New Testament love may prove ("self-sacrifice," "mutuality," "love for God," "love of the neighbor" — sometimes reformulated as "radical equal regard"), no reader of the New Testament can fail to note that authentic love is presented as both pure gift and radical command. Catholic interpreters will ordinarily also note that *agape* does not merely displace or destroy *eros* but — as in the incarnational and sacramental vision of John — transforms all *eros* into genuine *caritas*.

The exact nature of the model of transformation will also depend upon the particular (ordinarily the cultural) model for authentic *eros* which the theologian employs to understand the authentic *eros*-love of our ordinary experience. One may employ (as did Gregory of Nyssa) a neo-Platonic model with its metaphor of the purification of *eros* as one ascends "the ladder of love" from lesser loves to the reality of "spiritual" *eros* — love for the Loving God. One may employ (as did Thomas Aquinas) an Aristotelian model of authentic friendship to understand both our relationships to one another and to God. One may employ a model of courtly love, or romantic love, or some modern psychological model (Freud, Jung, Erikson, Fromm, and others) to understand the *eros* of our cultural experience. For example, many psychologically informed theologians today are anxious to understand the realities of "intimacy" among contemporary persons as an authentic and good *eros* model for loving actions and attitudes among human beings. There is always present some model of what the classical writers named "*eros*" to understand the reality of love in our lives — with all its giftedness, ecstasy, creativity, and ambiguity. Hence, contemporary Catholics, either implicitly or explicitly, attempt to understand and make their contributions from their cultural experience to the *caritas* synthesis of Catholic Christianity. By way of initial and tentative suggestions along these same lines, I will close with a discussion of one model of theological transformation as related to certain contemporary models of *eros*.

III. Transformation and Contemporary Self-Transcendence

From a Christian theological viewpoint, love may be recognized as the concrete experiential form of grace. For grace is the Christian theological word for describing the event, happening, gift of God's self-communication in creation and redemption. On the experiential side, the reality of grace is experienced in the pure giftedness of life itself and in the gift-experiences of the explicitly "theological virtues': faith, hope, and love. The reality of the giftedness of life can be and is experienced in such positive "limit-experiences" as a heightened consciousness of creativity, a fundamental trust in the very meaningfulness of our existence despite all threats, an abiding joy and a sense of life-enhancing joy in loyalty to an authentic cause of justice. The same experienced reality of pure giftedness is felt in the self-transcending power and force of all authentic human love: love of a tradition, a nation, a church, a cause greater than the self, love of persons — friends, family, "the neighbor," and God. The intensity of these experiences of love can range from the more ordinary experiences of our everyday sense of trust, creativity, and loyalty to those intensifications of these experiences of faith, hope, love which we call mystical states of consciousness.

For the Christian, all these experiences name not merely the gift, event, happening of the self's transcendence of its usual and often fairly lackluster consciousness but sheer grace, the experienced reality of God's self-communication to us in Jesus Christ. For the decisive communication, manifestation, revelation of that radical grace is, for the Christian, God's manifestation of both who we are and who God is in Jesus Christ. In Christ — and thereby in the word and sacrament of Christ's Church — we know the experience of pure gift by the word "grace." In allowing the reality of that gift into our conscious experience, we come to believe that reality itself, despite all indications to the contrary, is ultimately gracious; that the final reality with which we all must deal is neither our own pathetic attempts at self-salvation, nor the horror of life in all its masks, nor even the frightening reality of sin in our constant attempts to delude ourselves and others; rather that final reality is the hard, unyielding reality of the Pure Unbounded Love disclosed to us in God's revelation of who God is and who we are commanded and empowered to be in Christ Jesus.

Grace, therefore, is that gift; it is most clearly experienced in what Christians name radical faith, authentic hope and agapic love. As pure gift it transforms our ordinary experience in three principal ways. First, it displaces "our hearts of stone with hearts of flesh." It displaces our constant temptation to trap ourselves within the self, to refuse to let go of the self *curvatus in se* (turned in upon oneself), to refuse to believe, or hope, that we need not justify ourselves to God, to others, or to ourselves. Rather that radical forgiveness and acceptance is already given to us as the pure justifying grace of Jesus Christ.

Yet as the Catholic tradition has insisted, this crucial radical displacement process is neither the final nor the grounding reality of the transformative power of grace. We experience the displacement of our sin because we experience God's replacement of all our strivings — with the pure gift of that grace. When that experience is allowed full sway in the self, we may recognize both the empowering and ennobling reality of radical Christian self-sacrificial love (as in those best moments of our lives for one another; as, paradigmatically, in those we name "saints" and "witnesses"; as decisively in the self-sacrificial love disclosed in the Cross of Jesus Christ). We may also recognize the empowering and evocative experience of "mutual love" (as in those experiences of authentic community, friendship and intimacy, trust in and loyalty to this person, this group, this community, this cause). When that experience is more muted, for whatever conscious or unconscious reasons, then we must face and recognize the reality of the *command* to love God and neighbor. In experiences of true friendship, in authentic community, in real mutuality and self-sacrifice, we often do focus upon that command. For in those moments we actually experience — whether we name it so or not is here relatively secondary — the pure gift of God's grace in the gift of authentic, self-transcending love. And yet, as Kierkegaard so persuasively insists in his brilliant *Works of Love*, we also need the command to love the neighbor in all *eros*-love precisely since *eros* also involves our self-interest, and we may be tempted to forget, therefore, that our friend or lover is an other, that is to say, a neighbor.

At other times too we must listen to the command to love: the stranger, the broken community, the frightening God of our frightened selves, even the enemy; that command to love must come in such moments to the forefront of our consciousness. For the command is itself gift: we are commanded and thus are ennobled and empowered to fulfill the command. We can displace our frenzied attempts to justify and accept ourselves and others because we have already been justified and accepted in Jesus Christ; we can displace the self from the first place of attention because that self has already been replaced by the gift of God's agapic love and the freedom it gives in listening to and attempting to respond to the command to love.

And yet, in the Catholic tradition, this replacement-displacement movement of transformation must not be thought of in a merely extrinsic manner (as in some doctrines of "forensic justification"). For the self is not radically evil, utterly corrupt, hopelessly fallen. Rather that self, in the Catholic view, is wounded but not — short of an implausible complete turn to radical evil — utterly corrupt. All the strivings of the self, in sum, are not necessarily selfish. All self-interest is not mere self-aggrandizement. Rather the fidelity of the self in its striving for, yearning for, working for a better self, a purer love (its *eros*) — all this is not to be rejected as utter corruption, pure "works-righteousness." All authentic *eros*-love — the yearning of the human heart for authentic happiness as Augustine named it; the natural desire of our minds and hearts to see God, as Aquinas called it — is itself affirmed, transformed, and converted by God's *agape*.

The displacement-replacement process of transformation by God's grace in Jesus Christ both restores our weakened and wounded but real capacity for authentic *eros* and fulfills that constant, driving, powerful force of *eros*-love in all its forms. For *agape* discloses the reality of who God is (Pure Unbounded Love), and who we in fact are (graced, gifted, accepted persons loved by the God of Jesus Christ); for we are ennobled, empowered, commanded to love each other, the neighbor, in turn. The continuing transformation of all our *eros*-love by God's *agape* is what *caritas* finally is; *caritas* assumes that the strivings of *eros* are neither irrelevant nor evil in relationship to the gift of *agape*. More specifically, as Aquinas recognized, it is not irrelevant for the Christian to turn to the Aristotelian model of authentic friendship rather than to reject it as "pagan," "corrupt," "selfish." One can, in principle, transform that model of friendship or any *eros* model in the light of God's self-revelation in the *agape* of Jesus Christ.

In an age when Aristotle's model of friendship, Plato's model of the ascending ladder of *eros*, or Dante's model of courtly love is unlikely to present the major model for a contemporary self-understanding of the *eros* tradition, then it is both plausible and warranted for contemporary Christians to try to formulate a distinctly modern *eros* model in keeping with modern notions of authentic "intimacy." Thereby contemporary persons may be able to understand *eros* as they in fact experience it. If we focus upon some model (or models) of authentic intimacy as experienced in our world, as understood by the disciplines present in post-classical culture, as related to the classical models for *eros*-love present in the long and rich Catholic tradition, then one may hope that modern understandings of intimacy may themselves be transformed into some new and disclosive *caritas* synthesis that speaks to us and our contemporaries with the same power and truth that Augustine, Aquinas, and Dante could speak to and for their age.

Indeed, if one looks at North American culture, for example, one can find analogues to the theological models of identity, confrontation, and transformation outlined above (D. Browning). The secular analogue of the theological identity-model is the model of pure self-fulfillment widespread in American culture. What have been named (by cultural anthropologists) "cultures of joy" find ready acceptance in many aspects of the contemporary demand for genuine self-fulfillment. Nor is there any good theological reason for a tradition accepting a *caritas* model to reject the drive to self-fulfillment out of hand. Joy, creativity, ecstasy (a fulfilled self) are, after all, legitimate and enriching desires of the human spirit. Yet if only self-fulfillment is one's model for the self, then the route to the "New Narcissism," or the route (more radically stated) to the self *curvatus in se* seems all too close at hand.

The secular analogue of the confrontation model may be found in various models for a "culture of control." Indeed so frightened can some secular critics of our culture's seeming obsession with self-fulfillment become that a whole spectrum of positions (ranging from the chastened liberalism of the Freudian critic, Philip Rieff, to various forms of cultural neo-conservatism) has emerged to demand some new and secular form of a "culture of control." The demands in any society for self-discipline, even for a repression of some demands for self-fulfillment in the light of the common good, are as clearly needed in our culture as in any prior one. Indeed Freud himself well matched the pessimism of the later Augustine in his insisting upon discipline, even repression, to allow "civilization." A tradition that recognizes the reality of sin, the ambiguity of all our actions, the need for disciplined reflection and discernment in the stages of the spiritual life — in short, the Catholic theological tradition — should not hesitate to incorporate these legitimate criticisms into a Catholic vision of *caritas*. Yet just as the "cultures of joy" can too easily become "the new narcissism," so too the "culture of control" model may all too easily become a mere "return of the repressed, the resentful, the weak."

The most relatively adequate secular analogue to *caritas*-transformation, I believe, may be found in what might be named models of self-transcendence. In a manner analogous to the transformation demands recognizing both intellectual complexity and existential ambiguity, a model of self-transcendence sublates the genuine demands of both self-fulfillment and self-discipline. For self-transcendence preserves the reality of the self's drive to authentic fulfillment and the self's need for real discipline; it challenges and corrects the temptations of the first to narcissism and of the second to weak *ressentiment*; it sublates or transforms both into a model wherein both the self's fulfillment and its discipline may be found in the reality of authentic, consistent, and lasting self-transcendence.

It is no mere accident that many major contemporary Christian theologians employ some model of transformation allied with some secular paradigm of self-transcendence. In contemporary Catholic theology, for example, both Bernard Lonergan and Karl Rahner have developed particular models of both transformation and self-transcendence.

When Lonergan, for example, appeals to the need for intellectual, moral, and religious "conversion" for theologians, he means that the realities of cognitive, moral, and religious self-transcendence must be acknowledged. For in cognitive self-transcendence the authentic self transcends its own needs, fears, desires in critical and rigorous intellectual inquiry determined to discover what is the case, not what I would like to be the case. That same self may also move past the desires of mere satisfaction and the fears of resentment into a world of authentic values and enduring character in moral self-transcendence. That same self may find and respond to the gift of God's love "flooding our hearts" (Romans 5:5) and freeing us to become lovers of God and neighbor — in an unrestricted fashion in religious self-transcendence. Note here how the *eros* of inquiry and the call to true value are sublated (preserved, yet surpassed) in the higher synthesis of the agapic and erotic love of *caritas*. The authentic strivings and demands of every self for self-fulfillment (for what the classical writers called happiness) are respected and enhanced. The authentic need for discipline at every stage (in intellectual, moral, and spiritual struggle) is respected and enhanced. Yet all are sublated into a model of self-transcendence that represents, I believe, the clearest contemporary expression of the Catholic *caritas* synthesis.

The synthetic model of *caritas* — and its recognition of *eros* and *agape*, gift and command, self-transcendence and transformation — may serve as an appropriate Catholic theological model for reflection upon modern understandings of human intimacy. Yet to state the model is to state an ideal form for consideration, not an actualized reality; the hard work of refining, correcting, expanding, and realizing the new form which the *caritas* synthesis might take for our culture is at hand. And that is a task which only communal efforts and new envisionments of reality might yet allow.

BIBLIOGRAPHY

Aristotle. *Nicomachean Ethics* (Cambridge 1993).

Browning, D. *Pluralism and Personality: William James and Some Contemporary Cultures of Psychology* (Lewisburg 1980).

Burnaby, J. *Amor Dei: A Study of the Religion of St. Augustine* (London 1938).

Furnish, V. *The Love Command in the New Testament* (Nashville 1972).

Kegley, C. W. (ed.) *The Philosophy and Theology of Anders Nygren* (Carbondale 1970).

Lonergan, B. *Method in Theology* (New York 1980).

Luther, M. *Commentary on Romans* (St. Louis 1963).

_____. *Freedom of the Christian* (St. Louis 1963).

_____. *Lectures on Galatians* (St. Louis 1964).

Nygren, A. *Agape and Eros* (New York 1969).

Outka, G. *Agape: An Ethical Analysis* (New Haven 1975).

Plato. *Symposium* (Cambridge 1980).

Part Five

**Hermeneutical Issues
and Theology**

10

The Particularity and Universality of Christian Revelation

Revelation and Experience: The New Resources of Revised Theories of Hermeneutics and Experience

In the recent past of liberal and neo-orthodox Christian theologies, the doctrine of revelation assumed a primary role for reasons largely posed by the related problematics of epistemology and historical consciousness. From Troeltsch through Bultmann, Barth, and H. Richard Niebuhr among Protestant theologians, from the neo-scholastics through the earlier work of the phenomenological and/or transcendental Thomists, the doctrine of revelation was reformulated in distinct but related theologies of revelation. In retrospect, however — and with no disparagement of the permanent achievements of that extraordinary period in Christian theology — the concept of revelation in these theologies seems now too determined by legitimate but confining considerations for knowledge. The relationship of revelation to experience was present both implicitly and explicitly in these theologies. However, experience functioned in a secondary role in comparison to the problem of the need for universal concepts for a radically historical revelation.

The need for second-order, conceptual discourse for a doctrine of revelation was studied with care and precision. The contours of the actual first-order religious discourse of the Scriptures (prophetic, narrative, poetic, wisdom, proverbial, parabolic, letters, hymnic) were,

Source: *Concilium* 1978/3 (No. 113), *Revelation and Experience*, edited by Edward Schillebeeckx and Bas van Iersel.

with a few notable exceptions, left largely unthematized until the last fifteen years. The legitimate theological difficulties posed since Kant and Hegel on the exact relationships of *Vorstellung* and *Begriff* were decided largely in favor of a *Begrifflichkeit* now shorn of its Hegelian claims and related to different concepts of radical historicity. The concept of "experience" itself, once so central to the doctrines of revelation of the earlier Catholic Modernists and Liberal Protestants, went relatively unexplored for these different theologies of revelation. To be sure, most Christian theologians abandoned the earlier and narrower approach to revelation focusing upon propositional truths in favor of a more dynamic, more personalist, more biblical, and above all more historically conscious approach to revelation as event. Still, the complex relationships between the first-order discourse of the Scriptures and the originating experience of revelation was noted but seldom thematized. The search for first-order discourse for new contemporary experiences of continuing revelation in our continuing history went similarly unthematized. Most attention was devoted to the second-order search for conceptualities more appropriate to the problematics of how to define the definitiveness of the originating revelation events in the context of a continuing history.

The concerns of historical consciousness — as epitomized in Ernst Troeltsch's classical formulation of the problematic of the "absoluteness" of Christianity — united with the earlier epistemological and conceptual concerns to demand central attention from theologians. The theory of tradition as *traditio* expressed among Catholic theologians influenced by Blondel and Newman, and reformulated more recently by those hermeneutical theologians inspired by the philosopher Hans-Georg Gadamer, served to challenge the too narrow confines of Enlightenment models of modernity, concept, symbol, and experience. Yet even this rich resource of *traditio* sometimes narrowed the discussion of revelation by assuming a merely negative stance against the Enlightenment. Nor did several of the theologies of . revelation as tradition explicate the relationships between different orders of language and experience in the continuing tradition.

The newer hermeneutical and sociocritical analyses, however, have provided fresh resources for understanding the relationships between revelation (whether originating or continuing) and experience. This newer hermeneutic focused its major attention upon first-order discourse, thereby allowing a theological retrieval of the originating religious discourse of the Scriptures. As witnessed, for example, in the work of Paul Ricoeur, this analysis has allowed the *referent* of this first-order discourse (that is, as referring to a possible-mode-of-being-in-the-world not "behind" but "in front of" the text) to emerge only after a careful hermeneutical analysis (including the use of literary-critical and structuralist methods) of the *sense* of different genres. The analyses of the parables as both metaphor and narrative are merely the best-known examples of these new hermeneutical enterprises. This same hermeneutics has allowed an understanding of the complex relationships among such Old Testament first-order languages for revelation as prophecy, narrative, law, wisdom and hymnic discourse.

In sum, this hermeneutics has advanced the rethinking of the relationships between revelation and experience in three principal ways. First, the analyses of the sense and referent of first-order discourse have freed theologians to analyze the originating religious scriptural language — the language closest to the original experience of revelation — *before* proceeding to an analysis of second-order conceptual theological discourse (theologies *of* revelation). Second, the emphasis in hermeneutics upon the logicity of meaning in both sense and referent as hermeneutically prior to the meaning of the author, the context, or the original audience has been sound. In fact, this form of hermeneutics has displaced any remaining romantic theories of interpretation from their once dominant position without sacrificing the imperative demands of historicity. To try to employ some mysterious form of "empathy" to reexperience the author's experience or the original addressee's experience now seems a fruitless task for the interpretation of the experiential meaning of the text. To interpret the experiential referent of that text in direct relationship to the sense of the text now seems the proper route for analyzing the revelatory experiences disclosed by the first-order revelation-languages in the Scriptures. Third, the emphasis upon the referent as a possible-mode-of-being-in-the-world has focused new attention upon the role of the productive imagination in religious discourse and experience. In fact, one may state that the concern with imagination of Kant's Third Critique is now viewed as central for understanding revelation and experience. This remains noticeably different from the dominant epistemological and ethical concerns of the first two critiques pervasively present for earlier theologies of revelation. In sum, the recent forms of hermeneutics inspired by Gadamer and Ricoeur have focused on that originating first-order religious discourse of the Scriptures in such a manner that the originating religious experience *referred* to by the text can be explicated without naive and romantic appeals to the interpreter's "empathy" for the experience of the original author or for the experience of the original addressee of the text.

Moreover, as the work of J. B. Metz and Edward Schillebeeckx (among others) has shown, one need not fear that this hermeneutical emphasis upon the narrative core of Christian religious discourse over later conceptualities will remove the sociocritical power of that first-order discourse itself. The *memoria* of the suffering of the oppressed encapsulated in scriptural narratives, for example, assures that the memory of the *traditio* need never become merely conservative in the manner of some earlier theologies of revelation as tradition. For precisely that narrative core captures — as conceptual discourse alone cannot — the tensions of the disclosive and transformative power of the authentically Christian experience of God's revelation in the event of Jesus Christ as Lord.

These familiar, fruitful, largely European developments of hermeneutical and sociocritical analyses of the first-order scriptural discourse for the experience of revelation can be united, I believe, with the Anglo-American reformed notion of experience itself to provide new resources for the present question of revelation and experience.

European commentators sometimes assume that the Anglo-American emphasis upon experience in theology is at best merely commonsensical, at worst empiricist. The "verification" and "falsification" contributions of A. J. Ayer and Antony Flew may indeed lead one to this conclusion, as may some of the hermeneutically unsophisticated uses of story, symbol, and experience in some recent North American theologies. Still, the fact remains that a major Anglo-American tradition in philosophy and theology from Jonathan Edwards through William James, Charles Hartshorne, Alfred North Whitehead, the process theologies, and the various forms of Catholic and Protestant "empirical theologies" have consistently argued against both conceptualism and empiricism in favor of a wider and deeper notion of experience itself. In one of his now classical formulations, Whitehead insisted upon the need for a reformed subjectivist principle. His insistence was not exhausted by the more widespread negative move against a Cartesian substance-subject in favor of a dynamic social subject-in-process. Rather, Whitehead also insisted (and here he was and is joined by all other philosophers and theologians in this empirical tradition) that the notion of experience employed in philosophy and theology was badly in need of revision beyond its conceptualist and empiricist confines. Our experience is not, in fact, confined to the reports of our five senses, much less to experimental verification (that is, to empiricism). Prior to all sense-experience is the primordial, pervasive experience of the self as a self: active, in process, feeling, embodied, intrinsically social, radically related to all reality. This primordial experience (technically, the feeling of non-sensuous perception) is always present to the self — a presence rendered consciously available through both elementary and sophisticated (for example, Lilly experiments) methods of consciousness-raising.

That same revised notion of experience both expands the candidates for experience beyond empiricist confines to feeling, mood, body awareness, time-space awareness, relations as experienced, and so on, and radicalizes the experience of the self as a self beyond both empiricist and conceptualist limitations. Indeed, as several theologians have attempted to show, the revised notion of experience also encourages a heightened awareness-experience of the whole as now frightening, now trustworthy, now fascinating, now terrifying. These latter experiences may be named limit-experiences. Certain of these limit-experiences (including not only the more familiar Jasperian negative limit-situations of anxiety, guilt, death, but the more positive limit-experiences of fundamental trust in a meaning and order to the whole) disclose a religious-as-limit dimension to our everyday experience distinct from and grounding to our cultural, scientific, ethical, and aesthetic experience.

In more secularized human beings, this limit-experience of a religious dimension to one's everyday existence sometimes serves as the sole clue to the character of religious experience and thereby to all personal appropriation of the languages of revelation (Whitehead's own urbane and secular spirit was probably of this cast). For others, more exactly for those who possess any genuine lived-experience of an authentically living religious *traditio* grounded in a revelation, the possibilities for experiential religion are wider, deeper, and far more intense than the earlier shared experience of a religious-as-limit dimension to the everyday. Christian revelation can be experienced by Christians living in a real religious community and an authentically revelatory tradition first in the form of what Mircea Eliade has analyzed as "manifestations" (as in a vibrant sacramental life or in some of the "charismatic" experiences). That same intense experience of Christian revelation can also be found in what the kerygmatic theologians have analyzed as the faith experience of authentic proclamation. For Christians, revelatory limit-experiences of both manifestation and proclamation are available in the authentic lived-experience of church.

The same experience may be present, now in a reflectively mediated fashion, in the theological visions of the whole disclosed by the second-order languages of negative dialectics or of analogy (or, preferably, both). In any case, the intensity of the Christian revelation-experience is disclosive not only of a religious dimension to one's existence but of intense religious experiences disclosed, nourished, and transformed by the originating revelatory experience of Jesus Christ. That originating experience is present more immediately through the proclamation and the manifestations of an authentic sacramental, ecclesial life, including the struggle for justice in church and world. That same experience is present in more mediated forms through the critical reflection present in the second-order discourse of theologians. It is further intensified by the continuing presence of authentic witnesses to the reality of revelation in the community (Mother Teresa, Dorothy Day, Dom Helder Camara). Yet these experiential resources for rethinking the doctrine of revelation are best rendered *theologically* (as distinct from religiously) available, once a theory of the hermeneutics of first-order discourse has been united with a theory of tradition that includes a sociocritical dimension. Both resources are further strengthened when united to a revised theory of experience that takes one beyond the confines of both conceptualism and empiricism. Still, these new resources may reformulate but do not resolve the full problematic of revelation and experience. For that, one must see what possible light they may bring to bear upon the still pressing questions of the character of explicitly Christian revelation.

Particularity and Universality in Christian Revelation: Classic Texts and Events

To employ these hermeneutical and experiential resources fruitfully for explicitly Christian revelation, the theologian must also find an explicit category with which to analyze the claims of distinct religious texts. First, however, a negative comment: the problem of Christian particularity in revelation should not be confused with claims to exclusivity. In fact, the mainline Catholic tradition in theology, with its frequent appeals to the universal salvific will of God, has been relatively unplagued in recent years by claims to exclusivity for Christian revelation. Still the need to understand when and how Christian particularity is neither particularism nor exclusivity but can be universal, decisive, and inclusivist needs further exploration with the new resources outlined in the first part of this article

In harmony with the notion of hermeneutics advanced above, a category worth exploring is the notion of the classic text. In approaching classical texts, all careful persons make certain assumptions. Chief among those assumptions are the following: first, there exists a qualitative difference between a classic and a period piece; second, there exists an assumption that a classic, by definition, will always be in need of further interpretation in view of its need for renewed application to a particular situation: third, a classic, again by definition, is assumed to be any text that always has the power to transform the horizon of the interpreter and thereby disclose new meaning and experiential possibilities.

Although these assumptions possess a firm empirical basis in any culture, there remains the theoretical difficulty of explicating criteria to distinguish between particularity and particularism, between universality and a mere universalism. One may reject romantic notions of the classic with their somewhat desperate appeals to "genius" and individual taste while still insisting that the origins and genre of the genuine classic are always particular. For example, what could be more particular in origin and expression than James Joyce's *Ulysses*, a work expressing one day in the lives of three persons in Dublin (Bloomsday — 16 June 1904)? And yet that very particularity unites with a proper genre to disclose the universal relevance of this modern classic. The notion of a purely universalist literary classic is a notion best consigned to Enlightenment hopes become Enlightenment illusion. For the fact remains that all the great classics of our culture achieve their universality precisely through their particularity.

In the genuine classic, an unusual, even paradoxical tension of particularity and universality happens. First, there seems to occur an intensification-process in one's own experience. An individual explores the meaning of his or her own experience, own community, own tradition to that point of intensification wherein the desire for expression of the experience becomes necessity. At that point, a proper genre (poetry, narrative, autobiography, and so on) is discovered or invented to reexpress (or imitate in its true sense of *mimesis* as imaginative redescription) that experience with force. Then all persons can imaginatively experience the feeling-tones, the meaning, the disclosure of this new possible mode-of-being-in-the-world. The traditional need for the presence-in-tension of both energy and form, both passion and *logos* becomes, in the analogous paradox of the classic, the presence-in-tension of particularity and universality. Indeed the universality of the classic text occurs only when a sufficiently passionate, intense particular experience is driven to find its form, its *logos*, its genre, and its universality.

The religious classical text takes that same intensification process, that same alliance of *logos* with the risk of personal passion, a step further along the same intensification route. For then there occur those limit-experiences proper to religion and disclosive of, first, a religious dimension to our lives and then, yet more intensely, of the explicitly religious experiences of a particular revelation tradition. The classical Hebrew and Christian religious texts find the proper expression of their religious experience in that first-order discourse expressed in the genres of narrative, prophecy, wisdom, hymn, parable, and letter of the scriptures. Those genres do disclose, without loss of the full complexities and tensions of a religious passion, a genre-controlled referent. That referent remains a transformative revelatory experience expressive of the experiential contours, the paradoxical, challenging, even "scandalous" and "foolish" meanings of the Christian religious experience. These meanings are experienced as the now confronting, now appealing, always transformative Christian mode-of-being-in-the-world, radical faith, hope, and agapic love.

Theological classical texts have the more difficult task of allowing a second-order, reflective discourse to enter more explicitly into both the process and the genre, and thereby the experience. When the theologian's more conceptual language maintains a fidelity to both the originating religious language and the equally passionate demands of the authentic interests of critical reason, the same process of intensification of personal-particularity-become-disclosure-of-universality happens: for then, a new second-order discourse emerges to disclose through the mediation of reflection the same, now continuous and appealing, not discontinuous and confrontational Christian possibility for life.

As that master of suspicion upon all theological language, Soren Kierkegaard, insisted, the question of a proper genre for expressing authentic religious experience (for him indirect discourse through different genres and pseudonyms) is one too often overlooked by the "theologians." As Kierkegaard's own work also witnesses, the genre of passionate critical reflection is indispensable for the modern religious intellectual whose religious experience is more likely to be one of mediated second naiveté than one of immediate first naiveté.

Since even their most negative critics admit that the Old Testament and the New Testament contain classical religious texts, it seems fruitful to reformulate the problem of Christian particularity in the hermeneutical terms suggested above. For then we can witness how the Christian classics, like every classic, are indeed particular without being particularist, are in fact universal without being merely "lowest common denominator" universalist. Indeed, the Scriptures serve for the Christian as the classic judging and transforming all other classics — the *norma normans non normata* of all Christian religious and theological language. Is this really so puzzling unless one is enamored of a strange search for a universalism untouched by particularity? Indeed, to reject the highly particular experiences of passionate intensity which are the very lifeblood of our lives because they are somehow assumed to be merely "private" seems, at best, counterintuitive. Is one really to deny the deepest experiences of one's life — the experience of love for a particular person, the experience of religious nourishment in a particular community and tradition — because the experience seems somehow too particularist? Classical *logos* comes in and through passion; true form through energy; the right genre through the demands of intense personal, communal, or traditional experience; the Apollonian experience of tragedy in and through the Dionysian; the universal in and through the particular. To remove that particularity is to remove the very possibility for a personal experience of religious intensification whereby the universal meaning of the experience may be disclosed.

The same kind of analysis holds when one shifts one's attention from the text to the person referred to by the text — as when one moves from the parables of Jesus to the Jesus referred to by the parables or by all the later texts of the New Testament confessing Jesus Christ as Lord. For the originating Christian religious texts consistently refer throughout their myriad of genres and formulations not only to the religious experience of the Christian (radical faith, hope, and agapic love) but to this Jesus of Nazareth as the Christ, to this Christ as Lord, as disclosive, as revelatory of the one true God who may now be recognized with all the force of a decisive revelation as Love. That event of God's revelation in Christ Jesus is the transformative event of a person in and through whose message, life, death, and resurrection the definitive revelation of both who we are and who God is decisively happens. This scandal of particularity becomes a scandal of particularism only for one whose notion of experience disallows the testimony and witness of others as contributing to one's own experience. Yet such a person, to paraphrase Aristotle's analogous statement, is not a human being but either a god or a beast. For human beings to recognize the ethical call of the authentic interest of autonomous, critical reason is not to disallow disclosive and transformative testimony from others. Above all, it is not to disallow the testimony of a historical event — a life — which witnesses that the deepest possibility for human beings is in fact the impossible possibility of a life of authentically agapic love proclaimed and manifested as present now through God's self-disclosure in Jesus the Christ.

The category of the classic, therefore, should be extended beyond texts to those events and persons referred to (in front of, not behind) the text. The notion of experience outlined in the first section of this article not only allows but encourages the testimony of those particularly intensified experiences of events and persons whose classical status assures universal and revelatory status. It was not mere happenstance that William James, who helped to formulate the revised notion of experience, also sought in his *Varieties of Religious Experience* to search out the meaning of those most intense forms of religious experience, the mystic and the saint, as testimonies, in his language, to the "strenuous life" par excellence.

For anyone who has actually experienced the transformative possibility for human existence disclosed in Jesus the Christ, either more immediately through proclamation and manifestation, or more mediately through interpretation and critical reflection, that event has all the force of a decisive revelation of both God, one's self, and, indeed, the final meaning of the whole of reality. For those whose notion of experience is in fact empiricist, that event is likely to be expressed in a fundamentalist form — whether theistic or atheistic. For those whose notion of theological discourse discourages reflection upon the relationship between first-order religious discourse and second-order conceptual and reflective theological discourse, that event is likely to lead either to the Kierkegaardian comic dilemma of the Hegelian philosopher or the defensive *pathos* of the neo-scholastic conceptualist. For those whose notion of autonomy disallows the testimony of the authentic witness, martyr, saint, that event is likely to attempt a divorce between the event and person of God's revelation in Jesus Christ and the existential meanings of the texts expressing that event. For those, however, whose notion of experience is sufficiently wide to encourage an exploration of intense, old and new, religious experiences, and whose notion of hermeneutics is sufficiently sensitive to the intrinsic relationship between intense personal experience and its genre-expression in classical texts, events, and persons, then the seemingly tired and merely conceptual category "revelation" becomes authentically experiential. Then the decisiveness and universality of God's revelation in Christ Jesus is recognized as both particular and universal, neither particularist nor universalist. When those same persons allow the corrective truth of the sociocritical power of Christian revelation to play its central role, the temptation of hermeneutical theologies to retreat into a mere traditionalism will be disallowed and the temptation of empirical theologies to become merely individualist or weakly personalist in the manner of "the New Narcissism" will be disowned. The experience of revelation is always itself revelatory: the revelation of God in Christ Jesus is radically experiential; when it occurs it cannot but be decisive in its transformation of both self and world by the God thereby disclosed; it cannot but be universal and definitive. In the meantime, we are presently witnessing in theology the many paths of a strenuous pluralism. Along those paths we all struggle — through theories of experience, of genre, of hermeneutics, of tradition and critique — to find the reflective discourse equal to that same liberating meaning, that same disclosive and transformative possibility first expressed in the parables of Jesus and in the confessions of the New Testament community that Jesus Christ is Lord.

BIBLIOGRAPHICAL NOTES

For work referred to in this article, see:

Gadamer, Hans-Georg. *Wahrheit und Methode* (Tübingen 1965).

Ricoeur, Paul. *Interpretation Theory* (Fort Worth 1976).

_____. "Hermeneutic of the Idea of Revelation," *Harvard Theological Review*, vol. 70: 1-2 (January/April 1977).

Meland, Bernard E. (ed.) *The Future of Empirical Theology* (Chicago 1968).

For more extensive development and citation of the new resources, the reader may refer to my *The Analogical Imagination* (Crossroad, 1980) where the notions of "classic" texts, events, persons, and revelation are developed at length.

11

Reading the Bible

A Plurality of Readers
and a Possibility of a Shared Vision

I. A Common Confession and Historical-Critical Methods

The emphasis on literary-critical methods of reading the Bible has increased the already acute sense of the variety of possible readings of the Bible in our period. Indeed, as the fruitfulness of various literary-critical approaches to the reading of all texts has increased, the new readings of the Bible as literature have also increased greatly. In the meantime, of course, readers of the Bible find a great variety of readings available from earlier and contemporary historical-critical readings of the Bible. In sum, in the modern period, first historical criticism and now literary criticism have demonstrated the remarkable range of possible readings of the biblical texts.

At the same time, new ecclesial and theological readings of the Bible in different cultural, economic, and social settings in our period have also increased greatly; consider the powerful new readings of liberation, political, and feminist theologies alone as new context-dependent readings of the Bible. The central theological question has become how to understand anew, on theological grounds, the unity amidst so wide and potentially rich a diversity of readings.

For this reason, there has been renewed attention in our period to

Source: *Concilium* 1991/1, *The Bible and Its Readers*, edited by Wim Beuken, Sean Freyne, and Anton Weiler. "Reading the Bible" is a new title for this article.

two theological candidates for unity-amidst-diversity: the common Christian confession and the common Christian passion narrative. Is it possible that these two candidates *together* may function to show a pervasive unity of Christian theological understanding of the scriptures without in any way denying the need for great variety? This is the principal theological question provoked by attention to the remarkable new variety of scriptural readings of our period.

To begin with the common Christian confession:[1] the common confession is "We believe *in* Jesus Christ *with* the apostles." This means that the religious, revelatory event of Jesus Christ experienced in the present through word and sacrament is the same revelatory event witnessed by the original apostolic communities who wrote the New Testament. It is the revelatory event and not the witnessing texts which must play the central role in Christian self-understanding. And yet the "book," the scriptures, do play a major theological role. For the scriptures are nothing less than the authoritative witness to that event — a witness to which all later Christian communities hold themselves accountable. To believe *in* Jesus Christ *with* the apostles means, for the Christian, that every present personal and communal Christian belief *in* Jesus Christ is in fundamental continuity with the apostolic witness expressed in the "apostolic writings" become the Christian New Testament. To believe in Jesus Christ, moreover, is to believe *in* the God of Abraham, Isaac, and Jacob and thereby in the revelatory event of Sinai expressed in the Hebrew scriptures and now reinterpreted as the Christian Old Testament in the light of the Christ-event expressed in the apostolic writings.

The complexities intrinsic to any Christian theological interpretation of the scriptures becomes clear. For Christianity is not, strictly speaking, a religion of the book like Islam. And yet "the book" does play a central role for Christian self-understanding. Christianity, in more explicitly hermeneutical terms, is a religion of a revelatory event to which certain texts bear an authoritative witness.

It is difficult to exaggerate the importance of this distinction between event and text for Christian theological self-understanding. To fail to grasp the distinction is to lead into two opposite difficulties. To make the text into the revelation is to turn Christianity into a strict religion of the book on the model of the place of the Qur'an in Islam. Then the route to Christian fundamentalist readings of the scripture under the banner cries of "inerrancy" soon takes over. Here Christians believe, in effect, not *with* but *in* the apostles.

The opposite danger is equally devastating for Christian self-understanding: a removal of any authoritative role of the scriptural text in favor of only the contemporary experience of the present Christian community. It is not the case, of course, that such antitext positions are necessarily post-Christian. The difficulty is, rather, that since the scriptural texts are not allowed to play any authoritative role, the contemporary Christian community can never know whether its present witness to the Christ-event is in continuity with the original apostolic witness. The historical central Christian theological affirmation — "I believe in Jesus Christ with the apostles" — would then be narrowed into the affirmation "I believe in Jesus Christ."

Neither of these dangers has been present in the classic interpretations of the role of the Bible in the church. For despite their otherwise important, even radical, differences, all the classic mainline Christian interpreters maintained the hermeneutical distinction between the revelatory event of Jesus Christ and the scriptural texts as witnessing to that event. The text cannot replace the event to which it witnesses. At the same time, the interpretation of the event as present in later Christian communities cannot feel free to ignore its own continuity or lack of continuity to the authoritative witnessing apostolic texts.

It is worth noting that the scriptural texts themselves make the same theological point. These scriptural texts are, after all (as modern historical criticism has made clear), texts of witness by different Christian communities to the event of Jesus Christ. In that precise sense, the scriptures of the New Testament are the church's book.

The New Testament texts, moreover, are by any reading remarkably diverse in both form and content. The contrast between the genre of narrative in the Gospels and the genre of letter and exhortation in Paul, the clash in content between Paul and James, the contrast between the tensive quality of the apocalyptic strands of the New Testament and the almost relaxed stability in form of the Pastoral Epistles are differences whose productive possibilities theologians and exegetes are still investigating. What unites these remarkably pluralistic texts is not any single interpretation of the Christ-event (any particular "christology") but the revelatory and salvific event itself. What unites them is the explicit fact of witness by these early Christian communities to that Christ-event. What unites the New Testament, in sum, is the Christian community's faith in Jesus Christ as revelation and salvation. What unites later Christian communities to the early communities is the contemporary community's faith in that same Christ-event. What distinguishes the later community's witness from that of these early communities is solely but critically the later community's need to show how its interpretation of that same revelatory event is in continuity with the witness of the original communities. In short, what distinguishes the later community is the presence of the earlier communities' own witness as our scripture.

In this theological content, one cannot but continue to affirm modern historical-critical studies of the scriptural texts. For these studies have clarified the central theological points of the hermeneutical situation itself. These methods have provided historical-critical reconstructions of the original apostolic witness of the different communities (form criticism) and different redactors (redaction criticism). They have clarified both the different social settings (e.g., the brilliant historical and literary analyses of the import of Galilee)[2] and the diverse cultural historical settings of these communities in relationship to their situation. By focusing, for example, on the import of such historical events as the destruction of Jerusalem (70 CE), the Gentile mission, the persecution of the communities, as well as the difficulties occasioned by the event which did not come (the end-times), these historical-critical reconstructions have greatly clarified some of the situational reasons for the pluralism of interpretations of the Christ-event in the New Testament.

That remarkable modern series of historical-critical clarifications of the situational social, economic, and cultural pluralism of the early Christian communities has, in its turn, encouraged greater theological attentiveness to our own contemporary situational pluralism. That same historical-theological work has clarified anew the central insight that the scriptures are the church's book: products of and dependent upon the early Christian communities who composed them.

II. The Common Narrative and Literary-Critical Methods

Moreover, the common confession logically leads to the common passion narrative.[3] Literary criticism has helped us all to see how the Christian confesses not merely through the genre of confession but through affirming the passion narrative as the fuller meaning of that confession. The passion narrative shows us how and why the Christian community "believes *in* Jesus Christ" — a Jesus we find fully rendered only through the "realistic," "history-like" narrative rendering of the passion accounts. That narrative rendering, moreover, Christians also acknowledge as the plain, ecclesial (apostolic) sense of the passion accounts ("we believe *with* the apostles"). The common confession and the common narrative cohere in affirming that plain ecclesial sense (i.e., the obvious, direct meaning of these texts for the Christian community). But only the narrative can show, and not merely state (confess), who this Jesus Christ, present to us in word and sacrament, really is for the Christian community. This emphasis on narrative can also encourage a reappraisal of all the other New Testament genres — doctrine, confession, symbol, letter, commentary, meditative theological thinking (John), or dialectical theological thinking (Paul).

Modern literary-critical and hermeneutical studies have demonstrated the need and fruitfulness of these and other "genres" for Christian theological use. But all the other genres are helpfully related to both the common confession and the plain sense of the common passion narrative in order to affirm (or, in principle, to deny, i.e., *Sachkritik*) their Christian appropriateness. This is the substantive discovery of the new emphasis on the common narrative beyond (but in harmony with) the common confession. This position is not narratologically dependent on any particular theory of narrative for human life and thought. It is theologically dependent solely on the plain ecclesial meaning of the passion narrative as that meaning is further clarified by being analyzed as a history-like, realistic narrative.

A theologically informed narrative (plain) reading can also clarify how these gospel narratives, as gospel and not merely "story," are proclamatory narratives of apostolic witness to the proclamation of God's initiative in the event and person of Jesus Christ. Moreover, much could be gained and little lost by showing how these relatively late passion narratives with their "Jesus Christ kerygma" relate to the earliest apostolic witness of the historically reconstructed "Jesus-kerygma."

At the same time, it is the "plain meaning" of the passion narratives that not merely makes explicit the implicit christology of the Jesus kerygma but also renders in necessary narrative detail how and why the identity and presence of Jesus Christ is experienced as present to the Christian community then and now. If the Christian community means that "Christ" and the "Spirit" are present through proclamatory word and manifesting sacrament as well as through various Christian spiritualities of "presence," then theologically the Christian community should try to clarify how Christ is present as none other than this narratively identified *Jesus* the Christ and the

Spirit is present as the Spirit released by Jesus Christ. That identity is rendered through the interactions of character and circumstance in the narrative of the passion-resurrection of this one Jesus who is the Christ of God.

In sum, any Christian theology which confesses its faith in the presence of Jesus Christ (and the Spirit released by Christ) "with the apostles" will always theologically need the plain ecclesial (apostolic) sense of these narratives to achieve what neither symbol *alone*, nor doctrine *alone*, nor historical-critical reconstruction of the original apostolic witness *alone*, nor conceptual theology *alone*, nor confession *alone*, can achieve: a theological clarification of how the reality of Christ's presence is manifested through the identity of that Jesus rendered in the realistic, history-like narrative of the passion and resurrection: a narrative-confession of this one unsubstitutable Jesus of Nazareth who is the Christ of God.

III. Variety from Unity

The centrality of the plain sense of the passion narratives, moreover, should reopen rather than close Christian theological attention to other theological readings. As long as the plain sense of the passion narratives is understood as the fuller rendering of the common Christian confession, then a further diversity of readings of both confession and narrative will inevitably occur.

If one grants the importance of the common confession and the plain sense of the common passion narrative, then a further question occurs. Should the theologian also affirm: first, all the differences in the individual passion narratives; second, all the differences in all the other parts of the Gospels (the ministry and sayings); third, all the differences in all the other genres of the New Testament?

The different readings begin in the New Testament itself. It is, of course, an exaggeration to say (with Martin Kähler) that the Gospels are passion narratives with extended introductions. The truth in this famous saying is its insistence on the common passion narrative as the heart of the matter. The exaggeration is the seeming downplaying of their differences in the individual Gospels. The differences among the four Gospels are significant enough to demand a theological affirmation of real, i.e., Christian diversity. If one also includes not only the Gospels but also the other parts and genres of the New Testament, then the question of Christian diversity becomes unavoidable.

An opening to the individual Gospels is also an opening to the fuller story of Jesus beyond the passion account alone: his characteristic actions and his typical speech. The different synoptic accounts of Jesus' ministry, his actions and sayings, display to the alert reader how to understand a crucial presupposition of the passion narratives: the importance of the developing relationship through word and action of Jesus to the Reign of God and, thereby, to God. In literary-critical terms, the Gospel accounts of the ministry, moreover, provide the narrative details needed to assure that the relationship of Jesus and the Reign of God are embedded in the Christian consciousness while reading any of the passion narratives.

Consider, for example, the notable differences between Mark's interruptive, indeed apocalyptic, account of Jesus and the Reign of God and Luke's more temporally continuous, even "history of salvation," account. Since these redactional and theological differences also inform the differences in Mark and Luke in their distinct readings of the passion narrative itself, they call for further close literary-critical and theological readings of the entire Gospels.

Moreover, the same kind of differences have erupted through the centuries in the Christian consciousness in different pieties or spiritualities. It is hardly surprising that Mark's Gospel (which was of so little influence in the early church) now resonates so well with the kind of modern apocalyptic spirituality which informs certain contemporary theological readings of the plain sense of scripture — for example, the Markan "political theology" of J. B. Metz. It is also not surprising that Matthew's portrait of Jesus as the new Moses and his portrait of the church as the new Israel with a new Torah should have proved so influential in the early church — an emerging community concerned to develop its own institutional, doctrinal, and legal forms. Matthew has also proved deeply influential on the community-forming Christian descendants of the Radical Reformation — Mennonites, Amish, Church of the Brethren. Nor is it unusual that the Gospel of Luke (in its full narrative of both the ministry and the passion) allows for quite different Christian readings. Consider the appeals to Luke by charismatic and Pentecostal Christians focusing on the central role of "Spirit" in Luke. Consider, by way of contrast, how Christians focused on social justice tend to move instinctively to Luke with his clear "preference for the poor" (rather than Matthew's "poor in spirit").

Moreover, the Gospel of John has always been the favorite Gospel of Christian meditative thinkers — whether they be mystics or metaphysical theologians from Origen through Schleiermacher and Rahner. And Paul's renderings of the common gospel in the genre of letter and the conceptual forms appropriate to a profoundly dialectical theology of the cross have rightly been central to many Christians from Luther to Moltmann and Jungel. Nor do the Pastoral Epistles deserve Kasemann's pejorative dismissal of them as "Early Catholicism." Rather, the Pastoral Epistles (as well as aspects of Luke and Matthew) display a clearly Catholic sensibility where doctrine, institution, and tradition are prominent. The Book of Revelation, with its wondrous genius at excess, will always appeal to two different kinds of Christians: either those with a historical sense of persecution and present apocalypse; or those apophatic mystics (and, today, postmodern Christians) with natural instincts for excess, intensity, and nonclosure.

These brief examples of legitimately different Christian readings of the common confession and the common narrative may illustrate that there is no necessity to suspect that either the original Christian communities or the redactors who produced new readings abandoned the "plain sense" of the passion narratives. But can we really doubt that these different spiritualities, pieties, and theologies manifest a finally radical diversity of Christian readings of the common narrative? In sum, the common Christian confession and, more fully, the "plain sense" of the passion narrative should define but should not confine the possible range of Christian construals of the common narrative and confession. Further attention to the literary aspects of the texts united to the history of their reception, as suggested above, can show these realities of unity and diversity in the detail needed.

The too often underplayed literary aspects of both form criticism and redaction criticism also merit a new look. The productive, not merely taxonomic, nature of the genres analyzed by form critics suggests the need for further literary-critical and theological attention to how a particular text is formed through its genre and not merely how a particular historical context may be reconstructed by placing it taxonomically in a genre.[4] In redaction criticism, furthermore, the particularities of the differences also involved in the distinct Gospel accounts of the passion narratives have been further clarified by exegetes like Norman Perrin, who are not reluctant to use modern literary-critical methods of analysis.[5] Recall, for example, Perrin's brilliant contrast of Mark as an "apocalyptic drama" with Luke and

Matthew as distinct "foundation myths." These same kinds of redactional skills can allow biblical theologians to attend to the full Gospel narrative of the ministry of Jesus as narrative.

One initial way to assure contemporary theological self-critique in an emerging world church is to take the following step: keep grounded in the common confession and the plain sense of the common narrative, but also move beyond the common passion narrative to the whole of the New Testament Gospels and all other New Testament genres. Attention to the productive character of how genre renders content can help here. The Gospel of Mark, for example, can be read more as a "modernist" (in literary-critical terms) than as a "realistic" text. The non-closure of Mark 16:8 reveals the fear, uncertainty and hesitation that Mark's Gospel forces upon the attention of all careful readers — an uncertainty that "postmodernist" readers do not hesitate to embrace. The uncanny interruptions that disturb the Markan narrative consistently reveal both the apocalyptic sensibility and the strong spirituality of suffering as endurance of radical negativity. The disturbing inability of the Markan disciples to grasp the point of Jesus' words and actions at crucial points in the narrative as well as the pervasive motif of betrayal (Judas) and failure (Peter) should allow any sensitive reader to become hesitant to claim to understand too quickly this disturbing text through purely literary "realistic" genres.

Or consider another example: the Gospel of John is a narrative that is more like an oratorio.[6] For to read John attentively is more like listening to Handel's Messiah than it is like reading a realistic novel. The rhythmic character of this oratorio-like narrative with its brilliant use of signs and images (light-darkness, truth-falsehood, etc.), with its strange and pervasive irony, and with its meditative, disclosive, and iconic power, releases an attentive reader to meditate even while following the narrative. And was Luther so wrong to sense his own affinity to the genre of dialectic in Paul's theology of the crucified Christ? The tensive Pauline language of "so much more," "not yet," "and yet" released in Paul's relentless and unresolved dialectic is, of course, Jewish. Nevertheless, through his unique conceptual power, Paul dialectically rendered the searing centrality of Christ's cross into the Christian consciousness through his rethinking the passion narrative into the genre of dialectical thought.

As theological attention to the narratives and all the other genres of the New Testament expands, moreover, Christian theologians may learn further ways of reading the Hebrew scriptures as now, for the

Christian, the Old Testament. Note the illumination cast upon the liberation implications of the passion narrative when those narratives are read alongside the Exodus narrative — as in African-American spirituality and theology, or Latin American theologies of liberation. Or consider how Westermann's Christian theological reading of Genesis can inform the implications of the passion narrative for a new theology of nature. Or observe, with Eliade, how even the cross may be construed, without loss of Christian specificity, as also both the "cosmic tree" of a cosmic Christianity and the "tree of knowledge of good and evil" in Genesis. Or note how Paul Ricoeur's sensitive hermeneutical attention to the interplay of the genres of narrative and law, prophecy, wisdom, and praise in the Old Testament can clarify, on intertextual grounds, how Christians learn to "name God" more adequately by moving past the New Testament to the complex naming of God in the interplay of all the Old Testament genres.[7]

But all these examples serve only to make the central theological point: if diversity is not to become chaos, if unity is not to become mere uniformity, then the dialectic of the common confession and common narrative will always yield new namings of God and ourselves. Literary-critical analysis helps to show this by attention to *form* as often the key to content. Literary-critical readings have thereby joined historical-critical readings to show how the different forms are needed to express in different situations the shared Christian vision of Jesus Christ as the decisive disclosure of both God and humanity.

NOTES

1. For further discussion here, see Robert M. Grant with David Tracy, *A Short History of the Interpretation of the Bible* (London and Philadelphia 1984), pp. 174-87.

2. See Sean Freyne, *Galilee, Jesus and the Gospels: Literary Approaches and Historical Investigations* (Dublin 1988).

3. For further discussion here, see Hans Frei, *The Eclipse of Biblical Narrative: A Study in Eighteenth and Nineteenth Century Hermeneutics* (New Haven 1974); and, *The Identity of Jesus Christ: The Hermeneutical Bases of Dogmatic Theology* (1975); see also the essays in Frank McConnell (ed.), *The Bible and the Narrative Tradition* (Oxford 1986). Some of these reflections as well as further reflections may be found in "On Reading the Scriptures Theologically," in the 1990 *Festschrift* for George Lindbeck, Bruce D. Marshall (ed.),

Theology and Dialogue: Essays in Conversation with George Lindbeck (Notre Dame 1990).

4. On genre study for the Bible, see Mary Gerhart and James G. Williams (eds.), *Genre, Narrativity and Theology*, Semeia 43, Atlanta 1988.

5. Norman Perrin, *The New Testament: An Introduction*, New York 1974.

6. See Amos Wilder, *The Language of The Gospel: Early Christian Rhetoric*, New York and London 1964.

7. Paul Ricoeur, "Toward a Hermeneutic of the Idea of Revelation," in Lewis L. Mudge (ed.), *Essays on Biblical Interpretation*, Philadelphia 1980.

12

Beyond Foundationalism and Relativism

Hermeneutics and the New Ecumenism

I. Introduction: The New Europe and the Old Epistemology

That classic work of Western modernity, Edmund Husserl's *The Crisis of European Science*, is one of the last great texts of European intellectual self-confidence. But what a strange self-confidence Husserl possessed. On the one hand, Husserl insists that only a rigorous, apodictic form of phenomenology could save the "scientific" character of Western thought. On the other hand, Husserl argues — and here is the classic note of tragedy, that peculiar and extraordinary product of Western sensibility — that without such scientific rigor, European thought and culture would become merely one more anthropological type. For Husserl, non-European cultures can be adequately studied by anthropology, that Western discipline for understanding the non-European "other." One studies "Europe," however, only through the discipline of history for its past and the discipline of "social science" for its present. But one would never study "Europe" through anthropology — that is a discipline designed to help "us" understand "them."

The European theologians of modernity had their own form of a noble but ultimately tragic Western hubris. Adolf von Harnack spoke for many in his period of modern European self-confidence when he insisted that it was not necessary to study "other" religions — i.e.,

Source: *Concilium* 1992/2, *The New Europe: Challenge for Christians*, edited by Norbert Greinacher and Norbert Mette.

other than Christianity. For to understand Christianity for the historian-theologian von Harnack, after all, is to understand all religions. Some Christian theologians, of course, did attempt to understand "other" religions in order to understand Christianity itself better — like Schleiermacher and Hegel before Harnack, like Troeltsch and von Hügel after him. But even these exceptional thinkers usually had either explicit (Hegel, Schleiermacher) or implicit (von Hügel, early Troeltsch) developmental schemata designed to show in good, modern, European fashion how European Christianity is, of course, the highest religion. There are only a few European or non-European Christians who believe any longer in such developmental schemata, i.e., schemata with a secretly evolutionary sense of time and a culturally colonialist sense of space. The fact is that developmental notions are not the proper way to understand the relationship of Christianity to the other great religious traditions.[1] Indeed, more and more theologians, European as well as those in Africa, Asia, Oceania, and the Americas, now believe that all serious theology today will try to work out an adequate Christian theology only by trying to understand Christianity in culturally and politically non-Eurocentric ways. Perhaps only by trying to understand the meaning of the other great religions can a modern Christian achieve an appropriate Christian self-understanding in the late twentieth century. This latter "new ecumenism," moreover, needs to be worked out from the beginning of a theology and at every crucial moment in theology. The question of the "other religions" can no longer be left for an appendix to a theology.

The many new reflections, in Europe and by interested non-Europeans like myself, on the remarkable emergence of a "new Europe" may yet prove, paradoxically perhaps, a hopeful sign for all serious theology in a "world church" and a global community. For the "new Europe" clearly need not be a return of European hubris culturally, politically, or theologically. To be sure, some neoconservative theologians with their talk of a "Christian Europe" do sound disturbingly like Hilaire Belloc with his famous saying, "Europe is the faith and the faith is Europe." But even many neoconservative Eurocentric theologians do seem to sense that the new Europe should not mean the return of Christendom. Something else is happening in the thoughts of a "new Europe": a new modesty in celebrating difference and otherness amidst a new-found communality; a new experience of the vital traditions of self-criticism and ethical universalism of rights and justice, which "Europe" also means throughout the world.

Perhaps, after all, the new Europe with its noble hope for an ethical communality amidst cultural and political differences may paradoxically mean the end of Eurocentrism — even in theology. Perhaps, after all, the new multireligious and multicultural Europe may mean something very hopeful indeed. It may mean, first, the hope for a new kind of interreligious ecumenism as part of all Christian theological self-consciousness.

Second, it may mean the hope for a new kind of cross-cultural enrichment within Europe with its cultural and religious differences. Consider, for example, the possible difference to French — and thereby European — theology when the new Islamic reality in France (indeed, throughout the new Europe) becomes a central theological concern. Third, the new Europe may mean hope for a new kind of intellectual self-understanding where the brilliance and self-critical powers of European modes of thought can force European thought (including European theologies and philosophies) away from whatever remnants of Eurocentrism still remain in their self-understandings. The rest of the world looks once again to a post-colonialist Europe for new thoughts for the cultural and religious ecumenism which all theology needs. The rest of the world fears the reemergence of the kinds of old European nationalisms displayed anew in the former Yugoslavia as well as in the former Soviet Union.

II. The New Hermeneutics as Discourse Analysis: From Historical Context to Social Location

Let us reflect on each of these new hopes, starting with the new forms of the self-critical power of European thought. The reign of epistemology has ended in European philosophy and theology. The belief of the great moderns from Descartes through Husserl that philosophy can secure some sure, certain, presuppositionless "foundation" for all thought and thereby for all reality has collapsed. This peculiarly modern temptation — now named "foundationalism" — is in widespread dispute. The alternative, alas, is too often some form of postmodern relativism, whether explicit or implicit, whether self-confident or modest.

Hermeneutics has been one major alternative to both foundationalism and relativism. Hermeneutics has managed to take "historical context" with full seriousness and has thereby abandoned foundationalism without yielding to relativism. It is hardly surprising that so much European thought of our period is either hermeneutical in origin (like deconstructionism) or hermeneutical in intent if not name (like the dialogical thought of Bakhtin and many forms of East European and Central European semiotics and structuralism). Almost all present forms of Continental European thought attempt to be in conversation with, and sometimes in conflict with, contemporary European hermeneutics as the major twentieth-century intellectual expression of post-foundationalist but non-relativist European thought. Especially when hermeneutics is allied (see Habermas, Apel, Ricoeur) with some form of critical theory or some form of the "new pragmatism," the hope for an intellectual position beyond both foundationalism and relativism is genuine.[2] But many modern hermeneutical thinkers now believe that hermeneutics should be reformulated in our period by shifting the traditional hermeneutical emphases from "text" to "discourse," from "historical context" to "social location."

The shift from classical consciousness to historical consciousness, as Ernst Troeltsch and Bernard Lonergan argued in their distinct ways, was undoubtedly the major issue facing theology in the nineteenth and early twentieth centuries. Such historical consciousness, moreover, need not remain merely cultural and thereby idealist. Historical consciousness can also become (and has become, especially with the emergence of political, liberation, and feminist theologies) both cultural and economic, social and political. The development of new practical theologies in our period, moreover, has encouraged the same set of moves: first, from the individualism and idealism of earlier existentialist, personalist, and transcendental theologies and philosophies to a politically-oriented theology related to practical philosophies and to committed social, political, and religious *praxis*; second, from the earlier purely cultural analyses of historical consciousness to analyses related to social, political, and religious praxis.

In hermeneutical terms, this series of refinements of the meaning of historical consciousness and historicity had two principal consequences. First, there exists the widespread recovery of practical philosophies (such as Aristotelian notions of *phronesis*, virtue, and community; Hegelian and Marxist notions of praxis; the new North American and German neopragmatism as the necessary ally to hermeneutical theory). Second, there exist in post-Heideggerian and post-Gadamerian hermeneutics less purely culturalist notions of historicity. Indeed, the use of critical theory in Habermas as well as Ricoeur's development of a hermeneutics of suspicion (Freud, Marx, Nietzsche) to parallel Gadamer's earlier hermeneutics of retrieval may now justly be viewed as philosophical parallels to the emergence of political and practical theologies in our period.

To shift the language of hermeneutics from "historical context" to "social location" is simply to render yet more explicit the need for a hermeneutics of suspicion for every non-idealist philosophy and theology. All hermeneutics by definition take history seriously. All hermeneutics may also believe that a critique of conscious errors (encouraged by the hermeneutical model of conversation) is insufficient for all interpretive issues. But as political, liberation, and feminist theologies have clearly demonstrated, our problems *with* history (the tradition) and *in* history (our present social, economic, political, and ecclesial situation) are not confined to corrigible conscious errors (i.e., corrigible through better inquiry, better conversation, better argument, better hermeneutics of retrieval). Rather, our present problems include the need to suspect (the verb is accurate) that we are likely to find not merely conscious errors but also unconscious systemic illusions in all history, all tradition, all texts, all interpretations.

The language of "social location" (as distinct from the earlier, simpler, and too often purely culturalist and idealist language of "historical context") renders explicit this need for a hermeneutics of suspicion for all adequate interpretation. For to speak of the need to analyze "social location" is to insist on the need for explicit attention to gender, race, and class issues in all theological interpretation and all hermeneutics.

Any emphasis on social location can be properly viewed as a development of hermeneutics rather than a replacement of hermeneutics. On one count, however, hermeneutics itself must change: viz., by shifting its own emphasis from "text" to "discourse." [3] The focus on text in modern hermeneutics has become dangerous not only for its privileging of literate over preliterate cultures (the latter often revealingly labeled "prehistorical"), but also for the idealist and purely culturalist assumptions of the category "text." "Discourse," on the other hand, always demands attention to explicit or implicit power realities in the emergence of meaning and knowledge. For discourse not only means (as in Benveniste) "someone says something to someone" but also demands attention to forms of power operative in the someone, the something, the "to someone." Discourse analysis should not reduce meaning and knowledge to power relations. But discourse analysis also will not allow (as earlier forms of historical consciousness and hermeneutics could allow) an abstraction from the specific realities of power, especially the relationships of gender, class, and race: in all texts, all traditions, all interpretations, and all knowledge — and thereby in all theology.

Insofar as a hermeneutics of suspicion expands beyond the earlier psychoanalytical and revisionary Marxist models of the early Frankfurt school to some form of discourse analysis that deals with gender, race, and class issues (and preferably all three issues systemically related), then modern hermeneutical theology becomes yet more practical and ethical-political without ceasing to be fundamentally hermeneutical. For any form of discourse analysis that abandons its hermeneutical origins is likely to become either foundationalist (i.e., purely ideological) or implicitly relativist (as in much of Foucault and Foucault-inspired discourse analysis).

All hermeneutical forms of discourse analysis are (as liberation and feminist theologies implicitly are; as many other forms of practical theology explicitly are) neither foundationalist nor relativist in character. Liberation theology, for example, is, by its very emphasis on social-economic-political context, clearly non-foundationalist. At the same time, all forms of liberation theology correctly insist upon the implicit universality of the liberationist ethical appeal to justice. They are therefore not relativist, for justice, however rooted in context, must be universal or it cannot be just. The move, therefore, past a hermeneutical overconcern with "text" and "historical context" into a new hermeneutical concern with "social location" and "discourse" can be construed as a self-critical move within the non-foundationalist and non-relativist horizon of modern hermeneutics. Only when discourse analysis becomes either foundationalist (ideological) or relativist does it become anti-hermeneutical. Hermeneutics, thus reconstrued as hermeneutical discourse analysis, continues to seem the most representative form of European thought concerned to move beyond foundationalism and relativism

III. The New Ecumenism:
Christian Theology and the Discovery of the Other

The new Europe in a new world church also clearly calls for a new spiritual journey by all Christian theologians: into a new ecumenism where the other religious traditions become central to genuine Christian self-understanding; where the issue of the "other" becomes central to intra-European and global awareness. This interreligious consciousness first emerged in the non-European cultures of the new Asian and African Christian theologies; then in the rediscovery of indigenous traditions in the theologies of the Americas (especially African-American theologies in North America and the debate on "popular religion" in Latin America); that consciousness has now come full circle into the new interreligious consciousness of much European culture.

Many spiritual journeys are like the classic European journey of Ulysses: one wanders far and long but eventually returns home. However bad the trespassers who have usurped the old place, most at home remember one fondly; most even realize that Ulysses had to leave for a while; most do not demand an explanation. The journey of any Christian theology aware of the impact of other religions is a different one from the classical models for Western Christian odysseys. In the new Europe, as elsewhere, there is a new form of spiritual journey, new for Christianity and for all traditions in this late twentieth century. The new search is likely to become that of more and more religious persons: stay faithful to your own tradition; go deeper and deeper into its particularities; defend and clarify its identity. At the same time, wander, Ulysses-like, willingly, even eagerly, among other great traditions and ways; try to learn something of their beauty and truth; concentrate on their otherness and difference as the new route to communality.[4]

On the one hand, the new ecumenism agrees with the heart of all the classic religious journeys: the universal is to be found by embracing the particular. Indeed, those who break through to a universal religious message are always highly particular in both origin and expression. Surely this route through the particular is a wiser way to find truth than seeking that ever-elusive goal, a common denominator among the religions. Some people can speak Esperanto. Most of us would rather learn Spanish or Chinese or Arabic or English.

On the other hand, all religious thinkers today, while remaining faithful to the particular religious traditions which have nourished us with the spiritual truths through which we actually see and feel the world, should find new ways to learn from the other traditions. There are, to be sure, many religious thinkers who find it necessary to stay solely on one way, one path, one journey, one exclusive path to God — and give no attention to other ways. These same persons have their own Belloc-like versions of Europe as Christendom. There are still others who believe, sometimes seriously (as in Gandhi and John Hick), sometimes lazily, that all the great ways are merely different expressions of the same truth and the same goal; for example, from self-centeredness to Reality-centeredness.[5] The new ecumenism impelled by the new Europe is in search of some third way: you may find yourself and the truth of your tradition's way best by being grounded in self-respect while still exposing yourself fully to other ways, other journeys, other traditions. Near the end of his life, for example, Thomas Merton learned Zen practices and began to call himself a "self-transcending Christian." A similar leitmotif occurs through the interest in other religions among many theologians today who (directly contrary to von Harnack) believe that to understand even one's own tradition well, one must understand several traditions. Anyone who undertakes this journey must try to hold together three virtues ordinarily kept apart: the virtue of self-respect and self-dignity maintained by all those who never leave their tradition; the virtue of a radical openness to other and different traditions; the virtue of ethical universality with a sense of justice by all who insist upon the communality of the human. But what can the "new Europe" mean without that threefold sense of self-respect, openness to difference and otherness, and the ethical universality of true and liberating justice?

Today such new choices in Europe and throughout the globe are clearly necessary ones. For once any of us learns that we are in a tradition (cultural or religious), we can no longer be in that tradition the way we once were. Our choices then become stark: retrenchment (enter fundamentalism); flight (enter relativism); or what Paul Ricoeur nicely named a "second naiveté" toward one's tradition (enter critical philosophy and revisionary theology) allied to a genuine openness to otherness and difference. Ulysses-like, theologians need to wander: through modern critical approaches; through an exposure to other ways — religious, non-religious, antireligious. For many contemporary persons, there is no longer the possibility of a first naiveté toward one's own tradition and cultural home. The only serious question becomes: is a second naiveté possible? If so, how? Any of us may rediscover our traditions, i.e., experience a second naiveté toward its beauty and its truth, in and through discovering others, their difference, and their truth. But is it possible to honor the truth of one's own religious tradition while being genuinely open to other great ways as other? Clearly, the answer must be yes, or we are all lost in a Hobbesian state of the war of all against all.

The theological alternative is clear: a fidelity to the ever-greater God in a new cultural and religious situation where the realities of otherness and difference are critically and religiously appropriated by all Christian theologies that dare to move beyond any form of intellectual foundationalism and its institutional counterparts, cultural imperialism and ecclesial triumphalism, and beyond any exhausted model of liberal modernity that can promise only relativism. The emerging world church is newly anxious to be freed of Eurocentrism — freed by the theologies of the new Europe that struggles to find a new intercultural and interreligious theological identity for itself. European hermeneutics reconstrued as hermeneutical discourse analysis shows one way forward intellectually. Will the new European theologies show the same hermeneutical and political way forward in an increasingly multicultural and multireligious world?

NOTES

1. See Hans Küng, Josef von Ess, Heinrich von Stietencron, and Heinz Bechert, *Christianity and the World Religions* (London and New York 1985; Maryknoll, New York 1993).

2. See Richard J. Bernstein, *Beyond Objectivism and Relativism: Science, Hermeneutics and Praxis* (Philadelphia 1983); Richard Hollinger (ed.), *Hermeneutics and Praxis* (Notre Dame 1985); Price R. Wachterhauser (ed.), *Hermeneutics and Modern Philosophy* (Albany 1986).

3. On "text," see the groundbreaking study of Werner G. Jeanrond, *Text and Interpretation as Categories of Theological Thinking* (New York 1988).

4. For two expressions of this attempt, see John Cobb, *Beyond Dialogue: Toward a Mutual Transformation of Christianity and Buddhism* (Philadelphia 1982); David Tracy, *Dialogue with the Other: The Inter-Religious Dialogue* (Louvain 1990).

5. See John Hick, *An Interpretation of Religion: Human Responses to the Transcendent* (New Haven and London 1989).

Index